Choctaw Music and Dance

Choctaw
Music and Dance

By James H. Howard

and Victoria Lindsay Levine

Foreword by Bruno Nettl

University of Oklahoma Press : Norman and London

Other books by James Howard

(translator and editor) *The Warrior Who Killed Custer: The Personal Narrative of Chief Joseph White Bull* (Lincoln, Nebraska, 1968)
North American Indian Cultures (Stillwater, Oklahoma, 1978)
The Dakota or Sioux Indians: A Study in Human Ecology (Lincoln, Nebraska, 1980)
Shawnee! The Ceremonialism of a Native American Tribe and Its Cultural Background (Athens, Ohio, 1981)
(with Willie Lena) *Oklahoma Seminoles: Medicines, Magic, and Religion* (Norman, Oklahoma, 1984)

Library of Congress Cataloging-in-Publication Data

Howard, James Henri, 1925–1982
    Choctaw music and dance / by James H. Howard and Victoria Lindsay Levine ; foreword by Bruno Nettl.—1st ed.
        p.   cm.
    Includes bibliographical references.
    ISBN 0-8061-2225-0 (alk. paper)
    1. Choctaw Indians—Dances. 2. Choctaw Indians—Music. 3. Indians of North America—Mississippi—Dances. 4. Indians of North America—Oklahoma—Dances. 5. Indians of North America—Mississippi—Music. 6. Indians of North America—Oklahoma—Music. I. Levine, Victoria Lindsay, 1954–   II. Title.
    E99.C8H66   1989
    306.4'84'0899730762—dc20   89-40216

The paper in this book meets the guidelines for permanence and durability of the Committee on Production Guidelines for Book Longevity of the Council on Library Resources, Inc. ∞

2   3   4   5   6   7   8   9   10   11

Contents

Illustrations

Figures

Musical Examples

Musical Transcriptions

Foreword
By Bruno Nettl

James Howard was an unusual figure in American anthropology. Throughout his career he maintained certain central values of his discipline as they had been established by Franz Boas and his disciples, even while those values were being replaced by others in the approaches of many of his colleagues. His early publications were characterized by a holistic approach to the study of humanity and to human culture, the interrelationship of cultural domains, the confluence of history and ethnography; and so is the present work, which embodies major interests of his later years.

My acquaintance with Jim Howard goes back to 1953, when he was a graduate student at the University of Michigan and I a brand new instructor at Wayne State University. We met at the home of Gertrude Kurath, already a leading figure in dance research and the undisputed authority on American Indian dance, who wished to bring together young people with a variety of interests in music, dance, and culture. Having myself studied with George Herzog, C. F. Voegelin, and Harold Driver, I took it for granted that someone with an interest in American Indians would know something about their music and dance. Indeed, Jim Howard was knowledgeable, had much to say about peyote music (whose special character had just then for the first time been described by David McAllester), and, as it happened, criticized my avoidance of recent developments and mixed styles and genres in the Plains Indian traditions. It was a criticism whose significance became clear to me only later, as Howard was perhaps the first to point out the concept of "Pan-Indian" culture and then became a leading figure in interpreting it.

As ethnomusicologists developed their field and its approaches in the 1950s and 1960s, American anthropologists began to leave music totally to them, turning away from the Boasian embrace of the arts as central to culture. That this should have happened was probably inevitable in the light of increasing specialization within the anthropological discipline, but it was probably not a good thing. In any event, James Howard's career did not follow the trend. He maintained an interest in the study of music and dance, moving his focus from the Plains cultures to those of Southeastern origin in Oklahoma. And he worked to uncover the history of genres and events while documenting them in their present manifestations, thus upholding what I feel are important central values of anthropology.

In working on the project that resulted in the present work, Howard's desire was to provide an authoritative ethnography of Choctaw dance, with presentation and analysis of the music. Before his untimely death, he was able to engage Victoria Lindsay Levine, a young scholar of ethnomusicology and American Indian cultures, to do the technical work needed for presentation of the music in transcription and analysis. She has now also done additional editorial work to provide a coherent volume which, besides telling us much of importance about the dances of the Choctaw people, provides a model for the integration of music and dance with culture, past and recent. It is sad that James Howard is not with us to see the final product of this collaboration. But my long acquaintance with him convinces me that its character corresponds precisely to his ideas of how American Indian culture should be presented, and to his conception of the nature of anthropology.

Preface

My interest in Choctaw music and dance began in 1965 when I visited the Mississippi Choctaws in connection with research on the survival of prehistoric art motifs and architectural forms among historic and present-day Southeastern groups (cf. Howard 1968). In July of that year, assisted by my wife, Elfriede, and Kathleen Lynch, a graduate student, I spent several days interviewing Choctaw informants in and around Philadelphia, Mississippi, particularly in Bogue Chitto community. While there, we were privileged to attend a rehearsal of the Bogue Chitto dance troupe, which was practicing for the annual Choctaw Fair to be held later that summer from August 25 through 28. The Bogue Chitto troupe included Prentis Jackson, Bob Henry, Ida May Frazer, Henry Joe, Ovie Joe, and Tony Bell and their families. The troupe demonstrated their complete roster of dances for us and permitted me to tape the musical accompaniment. Older members of the troupe likewise answered questions regarding the names and symbolism of the dances. Ms. Lynch and I kept separate notebooks on these performances and interviews, and I have incorporated material from her notes in this monograph.

In 1974 my wife and I returned to Mississippi to attend that year's Choctaw Fair. On that occasion I did not record any music but instead concentrated on photographing and recording the choreography of the dances. The Choctaw Fair features dance performances by several troupes representing various Mississippi Choctaw communities, and we attended and took notes on every performance by each group. This proved to be an excellent opportunity to compare variations of the same dance as performed in different Mississippi Choctaw communities and also differences in the performance of the same dance by the same group on different occasions.

My work with Oklahoma Choctaw dance had begun earlier that same year when I attended performances of Choctaw
dances staged in connection with the Owa-Chitto Festival at
Beaver's Bend State Park, north of Broken Bow, Oklahoma, on
June 8, 1974. This was the first public performance of Choctaw
dances in this part of Oklahoma for at least a generation, and
several of the Choctaws in attendance commented that they
had never seen their tribe's dances before that occasion. One
mentioned that he had traveled several hundred miles expressly
to witness this historic revival. The dance troupe that performed on this occasion had been organized by the Reverend
D. Eugene Wilson of the Choctaw Larger Parish, United Presbyterian Church, of Wright City, Oklahoma. Wilson and his
group of Choctaw dancers, all from McCurtain County, Oklahoma, had learned their repertory of dances from their Mississippi Choctaw kinsmen and, in fact, had imported the late Tony
Bell, a Mississippi Choctaw singer whom I had met in 1965, to
sing for their performances. I presented a paper on this revival
of Oklahoma Choctaw dance at the 42nd International Congress
of Americanists in Paris in 1976. My paper, including descriptions of the dances performed by Wilson and his troupe, was
later published in the *Proceedings* of the Congress (Howard 1976).
    In 1978, I learned that another Oklahoma Choctaw dance
troupe had been formed in the western portion of Oklahoma's
Choctaw country. It was made up of Choctaws of the Sixtown "clan" from Marshall, Carter, and Bryan counties. These
Choctaws were soon joined by a number of Chickasaws from
Johnston County, Oklahoma. This troupe, which is known as
the Choctaw-Chickasaw Heritage Committee, was able to re-
cruit its own Choctaw and Chickasaw singers. These were
people who had participated in Choctaw and Chickasaw dances
before both tribes abandoned their music and dance about 1937.
I observed a performance by the group at the annual Seminole
Days celebration in Seminole, Oklahoma, in 1979 and later became well acquainted with Buster Ned, the chairman of the
committee; Adam Sampson, Bienum Pickens, and Ardis Mose,
the singers; and other members of the group. The Choctaw-
Chickasaw Heritage Committee's music and dance tradition
varies slightly from that found in Mississippi in that a drum is
customarily employed to provide rhythmic accompaniment

rather than claves or "striking sticks." Buster Ned and his group have since adopted me as an honorary member of their troupe and have permitted me to observe and to participate in several of their performances.

The two principal published sources on Choctaw music and dance are Bushnell's *The Choctaw of Bayou Lacomb, St. Tammany Parish, Louisiana* (1909) and Densmore's *Choctaw Music* (1943). Bushnell's brief ethnography of the now extinct Bayou Lacomb band contains fairly good descriptions of the dances of that Choctaw group, including transcriptions of three songs and three photographs of dances; hence it is quite useful for comparative purposes. Densmore's monograph, the only full-fledged study of Choctaw music, has transcriptions of sixty-nine Choctaw songs and much valuable material regarding their cultural matrix. Unfortunately, most of those songs were transcribed from the performance of a single individual, and thus the antiphonal responses so characteristic of Choctaw music, indeed of southeastern music in general, are not noted. Notes on the choreography of the various dances, some of which Densmore did not personally observe, are very fragmentary. Despite these drawbacks, Densmore's work contains much material not available elsewhere, such as the vocal and whistle music associated with the stickball game, bullet game songs, a hunting song, and the music of some obsolete dances.

Earlier descriptions of Choctaw dances, such as those contained in the anonymous *French Relation* (Swanton 1931: 243–70), Folsom (Cushman 1899), and Catlin (1844, 1913), tend to be so generalized that they are of little use for comparison and usually describe dances that are no longer performed.

The present work, then, derives largely from my work in Mississippi in 1965 and 1974, from my observations of Eugene Wilson's group in performances in 1974, and from my work with the Choctaw-Chickasaw Heritage Committee dancers in the period 1978–81. These descriptions have been compared with each other and with those in Bushnell's and Densmore's monographs. The result demonstrates both the general homogeneity of Choctaw music and dance and also some slight local diversity in regard to repertory, choreography, nomenclature, and the musical instruments employed for accompaniment.

JAMES H. HOWARD

I met James Howard for the first and only time at the 1980 annual meetings of the Society for Ethnomusicology. I had just begun graduate work at the University of Illinois at Urbana-Champaign and was only slightly acquainted with his work at the time. I certainly had no inkling that he would influence my development as an ethnomusicologist. Yet a year and a half later, when he sought a collaborator for his study of Choctaw music and dance, Jim contacted Bruno Nettl, who kindly recommended me for the job. After a cordial correspondence, Jim invited me to join in on the project. He sent me his manuscript and field recordings and asked me to transcribe several songs on which I could base a brief description of Choctaw music. Soon after he sent me these materials, Jim tragically passed away. His original manuscript has not been altered and is presented here as chapters 1 through 3. My contribution to the work consists of chapter 4 and the appended transcriptions.

Jim had a knack for recognizing intricate and significant issues in contemporary American Indian performance genres, and that is certainly the case in this study. Since I could not consult him as questions arose during my work with his recordings, I carried out fieldwork on my own among Oklahoma, Louisiana, and Mississippi Choctaw people during 1983 and 1985. I doubt that Jim expected me to become so involved with Choctaw music, but I like to think that he would have felt gratified to see his work provide immediate inspiration. That is, after all, part of a scholar's legacy, and Jim Howard's legacy is rich indeed.

Many individuals have contributed in a variety of ways to this work. I wish to thank the Choctaw people for their generous assistance and cooperation. I am especially indebted to all of the members of the Choctaw-Chickasaw Heritage Committee of Ardmore, Oklahoma; Buster Ned, chairman, and Adam Sampson, song leader, were particularly selfless with their expertise, source materials, and time. I am grateful to Claude Medford and Minnie Hand, who both contributed taped sources used here, and to Charlotte Heth, who provided many helpful suggestions on my chapter. I appreciate the good humor, tact, and diplomacy maintained by John Drayton and Patricia Dornbusch at the University of Oklahoma Press during difficult moments. Above all, I want to thank Bruno Nettl, Claire Farrer,

Mark Levine, and Lyle Lindsay for their friendly guidance, encouragement, and support. Finally, I am grateful to Jim Howard for getting me started on this project and to Elfriede Howard for so patiently seeing me through its completion.

VICTORIA LINDSAY LEVINE

Colorado Springs, Colorado

Introduction

The Choctaws are a large and well-known southeastern tribe, the subject of at least 250 books and scholarly articles. Their early importance to the French colonial dominion and relations between them and the French, Spaniards, and Americans have assured them an important place in American history. Their semisedentary, agricultural way of life and relative sophistication earned them designation as one of the "Five Civilized Tribes" of the Southeast. Like other Southeastern groups, however, Choctaw culture is known to the general public more for what it acquired from the whites than for its indigenous features.

In this short study we have undertaken to cover one small part of this deficiency, namely, to describe in detail the surviving dance forms among the Mississippi and Oklahoma Choctaws, especially as they have been practiced in the last seventeen years. The period 1965–82 is a most interesting one in Native American culture history, since it was during that period that the long-time trend toward an abandonment of Indian culture was dramatically reversed. For the Mississippi Choctaws this meant not only an increased awareness of and pride in their traditional Choctaw heritage, but also the awakening of a feeling of Pan-Indian solidarity. For Oklahoma Choctaws, whose abandonment of aboriginal forms was more advanced, it meant the revival of the language, the stickball game, and the Choctaw music and dance tradition. It also meant the adoption of certain "American Indian" but distinctly non-Choctaw forms from what has been termed the Oklahoma Pan-Indian culture (cf. Howard 1955, 1965). The civil rights movement and the resulting passage of the Civil Rights Act of 1964 were undoubtedly important contributing factors in this revival of "Indianness" among the Choctaws and the discrediting of the previous

"American melting pot" or "100 percent assimilation" model of behavior, but other influences leaning in the same direction can be isolated as well.

The Choctaw dance tradition shows some evidence of Euro-American acculturation. This is particularly evident in the dance costumes of both men and women, which are clearly derived from the dress of early white settlers. Because of this, many non-Indians who see Choctaws dance for the first time are disappointed. One also seeks in vain for such features as the bravado strutting and dazzling footwork of the Prairie-Plains "fancy" War Dance or the massed choruses and elaborate choreography and costuming of Pueblo dances. The Choctaws, as John R. Swanton once wrote, were "just folks." Thus, their surviving dances, though entirely appropriate to their southeastern environment and life-style, lack the spectacular quality found elsewhere in North America. Choctaw dances and their musical accompaniment were undoubtedly developed mainly for the pleasure of the performers, and this is still their primary purpose, though for the past several years in Mississippi, and since 1974 in Oklahoma, they have been used for exhibition at the annual Choctaw Fair in Mississippi and at similar events in Oklahoma.

The Choctaws themselves recognize that other tribes' dances are perhaps more colorful and better crowd pleasers than their own. Hence, Plains Indian singers and dancers are now brought to Mississippi at fair time to stage powwow-style dances, in which they are joined by some younger Choctaws wearing Plains-style costumes. Some Oklahoma Choctaws, likewise, in their search for "Indianness," have taken up the Prairie-Plains powwow complex. Fortunately for those of us interested in distinctively Choctaw music and dance, other Choctaws have chosen to perpetuate their own tribal tradition. It is this tradition that will be described in this book. We may be documenting a moribund form, for the future of Choctaw music and dance is equivocal, in spite of the recent revival of interest. Of the 17,400 Choctaws in Oklahoma, probably no more than 150 have ever participated in Choctaw dances, and the singers can be counted on the fingers of one hand. In Mississippi, with a Choctaw population of 4,000 but a stronger native tradition, there are probably 200 or so dancers and perhaps a dozen singers. So far as is known, none of the Louisiana Choctaw enclaves preserves a music and dance tradition at the present time.

Today's Choctaw singers and dancers, whether in Mississippi or Oklahoma, are uniformly Christian. This means that the religious dances that were presumably a part of their Green Corn Ceremony, dances analogous to the Ribbon Dance, Feather Dance, and Buffalo Dance of the Creeks, Seminoles, and Yuchis, were abandoned by the Choctaws early in the nineteenth century. What they have preserved is a series of social dances analogous to the "nighttime" dances of other southeastern groups. These are completely secular in nature, though they could be termed "ceremonial" in a loose sense, since they are a statement of native pride and identity.

The Mississippi Choctaws have apparently maintained the continuity of their music and dance tradition uninterrupted (though not unchanged) since prehistoric times. The Oklahoma Choctaws, although by far the larger group, had completely abandoned native music and dances by 1937, and the tradition was dead or dormant from that time until its revival in the early 1970s. Some Oklahoma Choctaws sought assistance from their Mississippi kinsmen in this revival, but one group was able to revive its tradition by using the talents of older people who had learned the dances and songs before 1937.

Phonetic Key

I have certain objections to the Choctaw alphabet employed by Byington in his *Dictionary of the Choctaw Language* (1915:x–xi). Nevertheless, because it is an established source, and in general use, and because the present study is only peripherally concerned with linguistic matters, I have used the Byington alphabet when native terms are required. I have, however, added two letters (indicated by asterisks below) for sounds not distinguished in Byington's system. These are definitely distinct phonetically from the sounds just above them. Whether they are phonemically important I cannot say.

a	as in *father*
ạ	as *u* in *tub*
b	as in English
ch	as in *church*
e	as in *they*
ɛ	as in *met**
f	as in English
h	as in English
i	as in *marine*
ι	as in *fit**
k	as in English
l	as in English
ł	called "an aspirated l" by Byington, this is actually a voiceless, dental-alveolar liquid
m	as in English
n	as in English
o	as in *note, go*
p	as in English
s	as in *sir*
sh	as in *shall*

t   as in English
u   as *oo* in *wool*
w   as in *war, we*
y   as in *you*
zh   as *z* in *azure*

Dipthongs

ai   as *i* in *pine*
au   as *ow* in *how*

Nasalized vowels

a^n
i^n
o^n
u^n

Choctaw Music and Dance

1. Historical Background

The first European mention of the Choctaws is by the Hernando de Soto chroniclers Rodrigo Ranjel and the Gentleman of Elvas, who speak of the "Apafalaya" chief and river and the "Pafallaya" province. These names evidently refer to the Choctaws, or a part of them, since the tribe was known to other southeastern groups as the Pans-falaya or "Long Hairs" (Swanton 1931:4). They were then, apparently, approximately in the territory of southeastern Mississippi, which they occupied when they were again visited by Europeans.

The Choctaws began to assume a prominent position in the politics of colonizing nations when the French first settled in Louisiana in 1699. Like the Creeks and Chickasaws, they were subjected to pressure from the Spaniards, English, and French, especially the last two nations. This pressure led to the development of factions within the tribe, one supporting the French and the other the English. Eventually these internal differences led to a tribal civil war, during which those Choctaws who supported the French interest, the Sixtowns, Chickasawhey, and Coosa groups, were finally successful, peace being made in 1750. The ascendancy of the English east of the Mississippi, secured by the peace of 1763, tended to remove remaining factional difficulties. With the Louisiana Purchase, the intriguing by rival European powers ended, and the Choctaws became subject to the laws of the United States. As a tribe the Choctaws have never been at war with the United States. Some Choctaw warriors joined the Red Stick Creeks in the Creek War of 1813, but the nation as a whole was kept out of anti-American alliances by the influence of their great chief Apushmataha.

Following the American Revolution, white settlers began pouring into the Choctaw country so rapidly that the Mississippi Territory was erected and Mississippi became one of the

United States in 1817. White settlers clamored for the rich Choctaw lands, and the tribe was forced to remove further west by the terms of the Treaty of Dancing Rabbit Creek, dated September 27 and 28, 1830. By this treaty the Choctaws were given a tract of land along the Red River, in what is now southeastern Oklahoma. The bulk of the tribe emigrated to this Indian Territory in 1831, 1832, and 1833. The first Choctaw emigrants suffered cruelly, but those who went later sowed their fields promptly, and hence the tribe as a whole experienced fewer hardships than the other tribes that traveled the Trail of Tears. Some Choctaws, for a variety of reasons, held on in their old territories in Mississippi and Louisiana, though bands of them straggled west to join their kinsmen from time to time: 1,000 in 1846, 1,619 in 1847, 118 in 1848, 547 in 1849, 388 in 1853, and more than 300 in 1854.

Mississippi Choctaws

The Treaty of Dancing Rabbit Creek provided that those Choctaws who consented to remove and give up their lands in Mississippi would share in annuities, other cash benefits, and other inducements. The treaty also provided that those who chose not to remove could remain in Mississippi. Each family head who remained would receive an allotment of 640 acres of land. Single persons over ten years of age were promised 320 acres, and those less than ten years old 160 acres of land. As it turned out, however, those Choctaws in Mississippi were discouraged from making application for their allotments, and of the twenty-five hundred Choctaws remaining, only 143 heads of families were actually allotted land.

In 1903 some fifteen hundred Mississippi Choctaws removed to the Indian Territory, leaving only one thousand in Mississippi. From this small group all of the present Mississippi Choctaws are descended, and have now increased to a population of approximately four thousand.

From 1860 to 1918 the life of the Mississippi Choctaws was largely a matter of sheer physical survival. They had little access to the law and were therefore bullied and intimidated with impunity by local whites. Of the 143 allottees, almost all lost their lands soon after allotment. These lands were either purchased for a very cheap price or acquired by local whites through fraud. With no land base of their own, the Choctaws led a hand-to-mouth existence as sharecroppers on white-owned land and through the sale of baskets made by their women. Regarded as the social equivalent of blacks, the Choctaws had no health services and, except in rare instances, no schools.

In 1915, when several hundred Choctaws died within a few months from influenza and pneumonia, the wretched existence of the Mississippi group in terms of inadequate food, clothing, and shelter finally came to the attention of the Bureau of Indian Affairs in Washington. An investigation the following year revealed the deplorable conditions prevailing among these people, and as a result Congress in 1918 appropriated the first federal funds for the establishment of federal day schools. In 1926 a federal hospital for medically indigent Choctaws was established. At present the Choctaw Indian Agency headquarters at Philadelphia, Mississippi, has under its jurisdiction all Indians in Mississippi and Louisiana. The agency maintains departments in administration, welfare, education, soil conservation, roads, credit, and arts and crafts.

It is generally conceded by anthropologists that the Mississippi Choctaws are more traditional than their Oklahoma kinsmen. This is particularly evident in the areas of arts and crafts, music, dance, language, and costume. Until the mid-1960s Mississippi Choctaw women wore their native dress daily, and men also wore native costume when attending church and on gala occasions. As late as 1933 some middle-aged women wore an elaborate face paint when going to town to sell baskets (cf. Densmore 1943:plate 12, left). The reasons for this cultural conservatism are undoubtedly closely tied to the group's struggle to survive as an ethnic group in a white-dominated, hostile, racist social environment. The Mississippi Choctaws, much smaller in number than the Oklahoma group, are a small island of Native Americans in a sea of whites and blacks. Not accepted by local whites, and refusing to be lumped with the black community, the Mississippi Choctaws have constantly sought to assert their separate Indian identity. Therefore, in Mississippi, native dress, language, dances, music, games, and crafts have had an important function as symbols of ethnic identity, and this function has served to foster their survival.

Oklahoma Choctaws

The Choctaws were the first of the five great southern tribes to move as a nation to the Indian Territory. The removal continued through the fall and winter seasons for three years (1831–34), the Indians traveling mostly on foot in parties of five hundred to one thousand, each under the supervision of federal agents and soldiers. Hundreds died on the way as a result of winter blizzards, epidemics of cholera and other diseases, lack of supplies, and accidents. Once they arrived in the Indian Territory, the Choctaws found that little provision had been made for them in the new country, and the death rate continued to be high for several years. In some instances whole communities of Choctaws were practically wiped out as a result of the removal and its aftermath.

The first permanent Choctaw settlements in the Indian Territory were in three general regions: northeast, southeast, and west. The northeast region extended along the Poteau River in present Le Flore County and along the Arkansas River in present Haskell County. The southeast region was on the tributaries of the Little River and on the Red River in present Mc-Curtain County, and the western region extended west from the Kiamichi River in present Choctaw County. These regions were organized into three politico-geographical districts with designated boundaries under the constitution of the Choctaw Nation on June 3, 1834 (Wright 1951:105).

The Choctaws in the Indian Territory had more opportunity to provide for the education of their children than did those who had remained in Mississippi and Louisiana. As early as 1838, twelve neighborhood schools were in operation in the Choctaw Nation. The teachers at these schools were paid from educational funds accumulated under treaty stipulation, and the children were supported by their parents. Some of these schools were operated at mission stations founded by the Presbyterian, Baptist, and Methodist church organizations. In 1841 the Choctaw General Council provided for the erection of buildings for Spencer Academy, a school for boys, which was about nine miles north of Doaksville. In 1842 the council established a system of boarding schools for both boys and girls to be maintained from the tribal school fund originating under the Treaty of Doak's

Stand (1820). Besides regular elementary and academic subjects, boys were trained in farm work and girls in household arts and sewing (Wright 1951:105–107). These schools were powerful instruments of white acculturation in the post-Removal period.

More economic opportunities were also available to the Choctaws in the west, and Eagletown, Doaksville, Skullyville (Choctaw Agency), Boggy Depot, Tamaha, Perryville, and Mayhew were all well-known trading centers in the nation before 1850. Some mixed-blood Choctaws conducted businesses or trading establishments at these places, usually in partnership with licensed white traders from the states (Wright 1951:107). Other mixed-bloods, and a few full-blood Choctaws, operated large farms or plantations using black slave labor after the manner of southern whites. Newspapers were published in both Choctaw and English at Doaksville and Boggy Depot. For the most part, however, these activities were carried on by the mixed-bloods. The full-bloods continued to support themselves as small farmers and husbandmen. The full-blood Choctaws lived on isolated farmsteads or in small communities in the eastern part of the nation, where they cultivated small fields and ran their livestock upon the open ranges. In most respects the life-style of the full-bloods resembled that practiced in Alabama, Mississippi, and Louisiana before Removal.

Stickball games and dances continued to be popular, although laws of the general council prohibited such activities on Sunday (Wright 1951:110). Games were matched between counties or districts of the nation in the summertime, and large crowds usually gathered to witness these exciting events. George Catlin, the famous artist, visited the western Choctaws and described and painted their activities. His account of a Choctaw stickball game and dances held near Skullyville in 1834 has become a classic. Since it is one of the most complete accounts, and contains our only descriptions of the Ball Play Dance and the Eagle Dance, both now long forgotten, I will quote it here in its entirety:

> Whilst I was staying at the Choctaw agency in the midst of their nation, it seemed to be a sort of season of amusements, a kind of holiday; when the whole tribe almost, were assembled around the establishment, and from day to day we were entertained

with some games or feats that were exceedingly amusing: horse-racing, dancing, wrestling, foot-racing, and ball-playing, were amongst the most exciting; and of all the catalogue, the most beautiful, was decidedly that of ball-playing. This wonderful game, which is the favourite one amongst all the tribes, and with these Southern tribes played exactly the same, can never be appreciated by those who are not happy enough to see it.

It is no uncommon occurrence for six or eight hundred or a thousand of these young men, to engage in a game of ball, with five or six times that number of spectators, of men, women and children, surrounding the ground, and looking on. And I pronounce such a scene, with its hundreds of Nature's most beautiful models, denuded, and painted of various colours, running and leaping into the air, in all the most extravagant and varied forms, in the desperate struggles for the ball, a school for the painter or sculptor, equal to any of those which ever inspired the hand of the artist in the Olympian games or the Roman forum.

I have made it an uniform rule, whilst in the Indian country, to attend every ball-play I could hear of, if I could do it by riding a distance of twenty or thirty miles; and my usual custom has been on such occasions, to straddle the back of my horse, and look on to the best advantage. In this way I have sat, and oftentimes reclined, and almost dropped from my horse's back, with irresistible laughter at the succession of droll tricks, and kicks and scuffles which ensue, in the almost superhuman struggles for the ball. These plays generally commence at nine o'clock, or near it, in the morning; and I have more than once balanced myself on my pony, from that time till near sundown, without more than one minute of intermission at a time, before the game has been decided.

It is impossible for pen and ink alone, or brushes, or even with their combined efforts, to give more than a *caricature* of such a scene; but such as I have been able to do, I have put upon the canvass, and in the slight outlines which I have here attached . . . taken from those paintings, (for the colouring to which the reader must look to my pen,) I will convey as correct an account as I can, and leave the reader to imagine the rest; or to look to *other books* for what I may have omitted.

While at the Choctaw agency it was announced, that there was to be a great play on a certain day, within a few miles, on which occasion I attended, and made the three sketches which are hereto annexed; and also the following entry in my note-book, which I literally copy out.

"Monday afternoon at three, o'clock, I rode out with Lieutenants S. and M., to a very pretty prairie, about six miles distant, to the ball-play-ground of the Choctaws, where we found several thousand Indians encamped. There were two points of timber about a half a mile apart, in which the two parties for the play, with their respective families and friends, were encamped; and lying between them, the prairie on which the game was to be played. My companions and myself, although we had been apprised, that to see the whole of the ball-play, we must remain on the ground all the night previous, had brought nothing to sleep upon, resolving to keep our eyes open, and see what transpired through the night. During the afternoon, we loitered about amongst the different tents and shantees of the two encampments, and afterwards, at sundown, witnessed the ceremony of measuring out the ground, and erecting the "byes" or goals which were to guide the play. Each party had their goal made with two upright posts, about 25 feet high and six feet apart, set firm in the ground, with a pole across at the top. These goals were about forty or fifty rods apart; and at a point just half way between, was another small stake, driven down, where the ball was to be thrown up at the firing of a gun, to be struggled for by the players. All this preparation was made by some old men, who were, it seems, selected to be the judges of the play, who drew a line from one bye to the other; to which directly came from the woods, on both sides, a great concourse of women and old men, boys and girls, and dogs and horses, where bets were to be made on the play. The betting was all done across this line, and seemed to be chiefly left to the women, who seemed to have martialled out a little of everything that their houses and their fields possessed. Goods and chattels—knives—dresses—blankets—pots and kettles—dogs and horses, and guns; and all were placed in the possession of *stake-holders,* who sat by them, and watched them on the ground all night, preparatory to the play.

The sticks with which this tribe play, are bent into an oblong hoop at the end, with a sort of slight web of small thongs tied across, to prevent the ball from passing through. The players hold one of these in each hand, and by leaping into the air, they catch the ball between the two nettings and throw it, without being allowed to strike it, or catch it in their hands.

The mode in which these sticks are constructed and used, will be seen in the portrait of *Tullock-chish-ko* (he who drinks the juice of the stone), the most distinguished player of the Choctaw nation represented in his ball-play dress, with his ball-sticks in his hands. In every ball-play of these people, it is a rule of the play, that no man shall wear moccasins on his feet, or any other dress than his breech-cloth around his waist, with a beautiful bead belt, and a "tail," made of white horsehair or quills, and a "mane" on the neck, of horsehair dyed of various colours.

This game had been arranged and "made up," three or four months before the parties met to play it, and in the following manner:—The two champions who led the two parties, and had the alternate choosing of the players through the whole tribe, sent runners, with the ball-sticks most fantastically ornamented with ribbons and red paint, to be touched by each one of the chosen players; who thereby agreed to be on the spot at the appointed time and ready for the play. The ground having been all prepared and preliminaries of the game all settled, and the bettings all made, and goods all "staked," night came on without the appearance of any players on the ground. But soon after dark, a procession of lighted flambeaux was seen coming from each encampment, to the ground where the players assembled around their respective byes; and at the beat of the drums and chaunts of the women, each party of players commenced the "ball-play dance." Each party danced for a quarter of an hour around their respective byes, in their ball-play dress; rattling their ball-sticks together in the most violent manner, and all singing as loud as they could raise their voices; whilst the women of each party, who had their goods at stake, formed into two rows on the line between the two parties of players, and danced also, in an uniform step, and all their voices joined in chaunts to the Great Spirit; in which they were soliciting his favour in deciding the game to their advantage; and also encouraging the players to exert every power they possessed, in the struggle that was to ensue. In the mean time, four old *medicine-men,* who were to have the starting of the ball, and who were to be judges of the play, were seated at the point where the ball was to be started; and busily smoking to the Great Spirit for their success in judging rightly, and impartially, between the parties in so important an affair.

This dance was one of the most picturesque scenes imaginable, and was repeated at intervals of every half hour during the night, and exactly in the same manner; so that the players were certainly awake all the night, and arranged in their appropriate dress, prepared for the play which was to commence at nine o'clock the next morning. In the morning, at the hour, the two parties and all their friends, were drawn out and over the ground; when at length the game commenced, by the judges throwing up the ball at the firing of a gun; when an instant struggle ensued between the players, who were some six or seven hundred in numbers, and were mutually endeavouring to catch the ball in their sticks, and throw it home and between their respective stakes; which, whenever successfully done, counts one for game. In this game every player was dressed alike, that is, *divested* of all dress, except the girdle and the tail, which I have before described; and in these desperate struggles for the ball, when it is *up* (where hundreds are running together and leaping, actually over each other's heads, and darting between their adversaries' legs, tripping and throwing, and foiling each other in every possible manner, and every voice raised to the highest key, in shrill yelps and barks): there are rapid successions of feats, and of incidents, that astonish and amuse far beyond the conception of any one who has not had the singular good luck to witness them. In these struggles, every mode is used that can be devised, to oppose the progress of the foremost, who is likely to get the ball; and these obstructions often meet desperate individual resistance, which terminates in a violent scuffle, and sometimes in fisticuffs; when their sticks are dropped, and the parties are unmolested, whilst they are settling it between themselves; unless it be by a general *stampedo,* to which they are subject who are down, if the ball happens to pass in their direction. Every weapon, by a rule of all ball-plays, is laid by in their respective encampments, and no man allowed to go for one; so that the sudden broils that take place on the ground, are presumed to be as suddenly settled without any probability of much personal injury; and no one is allowed to interfere in any way with the contentious individuals.

There are times, when the ball gets to the ground, and such a confused mass rushing together around it, and knocking their sticks together, without the possibility of any one getting or seeing it, for the dust that they raise, that the spectator loses his strength, and everything else but his senses; when the condensed mass of ball-sticks, and shins, and bloody noses, is carried around the different parts of the ground, for a quarter of an hour at a time, without any one of the mass being able to see the ball; and which they are often thus scuffling for, several minutes after it has been thrown off, and played over another part of the ground.

For each time that the ball was passed between the stakes of either party, one was counted for their game, and a halt of about one minute; when it was again started by the judges of the play, and a similar struggle ensued; and so on until the successful party arrived to 100, which was the limit of the game, and accomplished at an hour's sun, when they took the stakes; and then, by a previous agreement, produced a number of jugs of whiskey, which gave all a wholesome drink, and sent them all off merry and in good humour, but not drunk.

After this exciting day, the concourse was assembled in the vicinity of the agency house, where we had a great variety of dances and other amusements; the most of which I have described on former occasions. One, however, was new to me, and I must say a few words of it: this was the *Eagle Dance,* a very pretty scene, which is got up by their young men, in honour of that bird, for which they seem to have a religious regard. This picturesque dance was given by twelve or sixteen men, whose bodies were chiefly naked and painted white, with white clay, and each one holding in his hand the tail of the eagle, while his head was also decorated with an eagle's quill. Spears were stuck in the ground, around which the dance was performed by four men at a time, who had simultaneously, at the beat of the drum, jumped up from the ground where they had all sat in rows of four, one row immediately behind the other, and ready to take the place of the first four when they left the ground fatigued, which they did by hopping or jumping around behind the rest, and taking their seats, ready to come up again in their turn, after each of the other sets had been through the same forms.

In this dance, the steps or rather jumps, were different from anything I had ever witnessed before, as the dancers were squat down, with their bodies almost to the ground, in a severe and most difficult posture, as will have been seen in the drawing. [Catlin 1844, II:123–27]

It is unfortunate that Catlin failed to describe, with the sole exception of the Eagle Dance, the "great variety of dances and other amusements" that he witnessed at the Choctaw Agency, as some of the dances were undoubtedly early forms of those still performed by Choctaws in Mississippi and Oklahoma. Following Catlin's visit, the record falls silent in respect to Oklahoma Choctaw dances. A careful search of the published literature and numerous archival sources has failed to uncover any other traveler's or historian's account of Oklahoma Choctaw dances, though we know they continued to be performed.

Certainly during the latter half of the nineteenth century and the first half of the twentieth the Oklahoma Choctaws were undergoing rapid white acculturation. A part of this process was the conscious abandonment of traditional forms of religious worship, native dress, and dance—in short, an all-out effort to remodel their culture to approximate that of the whites. In some Choctaw families this ultra-assimilationist sentiment was even extended to the use of the Choctaw language. Thus, in a speech at the National Conference for Teachers of Indian Students held in Lawton, Oklahoma, in July 1972, James Belvin, principal chief of the Oklahoma Choctaws, stated that his father had instructed him when he was a very small boy never to learn the Choctaw language, since it would only handicap him in later life. He followed his father's advice and refused to learn his native tongue.

The traditional stickball games, as described by Catlin, managed to survive into the 1930s, but even they eventually disappeared. Even before Removal, most Choctaws had converted to Christianity, and in their new home in the Indian Territory the church became the focal point of Choctaw community life. Traditional Indian dances, since they were connected either directly or indirectly with the older "pagan" forms of worship, such as the Green Corn Ceremony, were often singled out for condemnation by both white missionaries and native Choctaw ministers. Such activities were considered to be the "work of the devil," and participation in them was evidence of "backsliding." Though the historical record is sketchy, this assimilationist sentiment and the opposition of the church would seem to explain the disappearance, at least as a public phenomenon, of traditional Indian dances among the Oklahoma Choctaws. Thus Muriel Wright, in her *Guide to the Indian Tribes of Oklahoma*, published in 1951, reported: "Choctaw tribal dances are no longer held in Oklahoma. Choctaw ball games and some old customs are now seen only as a part of educational and entertainment programs given by the Choctaw schools to present tribal history" (Wright 1951:118).

Statements of Oklahoma Choctaw informants and whites who have grown up in the Choctaw country indicate that in a few Oklahoma Choctaw communities traditional dances continued to be performed well into the twentieth century. Apparently this was often done *sub rosa* for fear of criticism by native Christian ministers. Tribal officials likewise discouraged such activities. Buster Ned, chairman of the Choctaw-Chickasaw Heritage Committee, recalls that his grandfather, Logan Parker, was one of the leaders in Choctaw dances and stickball games held in the Ardmore, Oklahoma, area in the period 1919–37. His home, southeast of Mannsville, Oklahoma, was one and a half miles northeast of the Yellow Hills dance ground. Other dance leaders of that era were Emile Scott, Joe Pickens (Chickasaw), C. S. Tubbee, Jack Williams, Charley Lewis, Flex Johnson, Johnny Gilmore, John Sampson, and Billy Washington. By 1937, however, opposition to such activities by "church people" had become so intense that the remaining dancers and singers decided to "put the dancing to sleep." From that time until 1974, the dance tradition of the Oklahoma Choctaws was for all intents and purposes dead. Many of my Choctaw students at Oklahoma State University in the period 1968–74 were completely unaware that their people had ever possessed Indian dances of their own, and inquired about this seeming lack in class discussions, wondering why the Choctaws were so different from other Indians in that respect. At that point it appeared to many, as it had to Muriel Wright, that the acculturation of the Oklahoma Choctaws was virtually complete.

Cultural Revival

In the late 1960s and early 1970s many of the youth and younger adults among the Oklahoma Choctaws began to be stirred by the new "Indian awareness" that was affecting Native Americans throughout North America. This movement manifested itself in many ways. For some Choctaws, participation in all-Indian gospel singing groups or all-Indian athletic teams was deemed sufficient as a means of expressing Indian identity. Other Oklahoma Choctaws sought to reaffirm their ethnicity by participating in the Pan-Indian powwow complex, joining in the Plains Indian–derived War Dance and Gourd Dance under the tutelage of their Kiowa, Comanche, and Ponca friends. One such Choctaw is Frank Watson, who is an enthusiastic dancer in the "straight" War Dance tradition. Frank actively participates in the Comanche, Kiowa, Ponca, and other Plains tribes' dances and has attempted, though with indifferent success, to sponsor Pan-Indian powwows in the Choctaw area of Oklahoma and to interest his fellow tribesmen in the powwow complex.

For other Oklahoma Choctaws, neither of these routes was acceptable, since both are ultimately non-Choctaw in origin, so some of these seekers after their cultural roots began to revive Choctaw music and dance in Oklahoma. One leader of the Choctaw dance revival in Oklahoma is the Reverend D. Eugene Wilson of the Choctaw Larger Parish, United Presbyterian Church. Wilson, who resides in Idabel, told me in 1974 that he was interested in developing an activity among Choctaw young people that would provide wholesome recreation and at the same time emphasize the distinct cultural heritage of the Choctaws. He therefore recruited a company of dancers who felt as he did, and the group developed a repertory of native dances for public performance.

Wilson's group learned their dances by observing performances at the Mississippi Choctaw Fair and by instruction from Mississippi Choctaw teachers. For their first public performance, which took place at the 1974 Owa-Chitto Festival at Beaver's Bend State Park, near Broken Bow, Oklahoma, a Mississippi Choctaw singer, the late Tony Bell of Bogue Chitto community, was imported to sing for the group. Later that same summer, Wilson and his group performed for their kinsmen in the Choctaw community near Jena, Louisiana. The Jena Choctaws are another group that has lost its native music and dance tradition.

The second group of Oklahoma Choctaw dancers known to me is that led by the aforementioned Buster Ned of Mannsville, Oklahoma, in the western part of Oklahoma's Choctaw country. As a boy, Ned participated in the last dances and stickball games at the Yellow Hills dance ground when his grandfather, Logan Parker, was a prominent leader. He left Oklahoma shortly before World War II and made a career in the Marine Corps. While in the Marines he would occasionally meet other Choctaws, and they would visit about boyhood days in Oklahoma. These reminiscences made Ned resolve that when he retired from the service, he would gather about him others of a like mind and revive the Choctaw dance tradition in his part of Oklahoma.

This he has done, in spite of considerable opposition from some Choctaws and local whites. The group of which he is chairman and prime mover includes both Choctaws of the Sixtown "clan" or local group and a number of Chickasaws and calls itself the Choctaw-Chickasaw Heritage Committee. It is fortunate to have its own singers, including Choctaws Adam Sampson and Ned and Chickasaw Bienum Pickens. In addition to holding private dance events, the group travels widely, staging performances at Indian gatherings and for white audiences in Oklahoma and Texas, and it has even issued two record albums. The Choctaw-Chickasaw Heritage Committee dance troupe, henceforth referred to as either Buster Ned's troupe or the Sixtown troupe, is the only Choctaw dance group whose singers customarily use a hand drum, rather than claves, to accompany their songs. Buster is particularly proud of the way in which his group's dancers respond antiphonally to the leader's songs.

2. *Performance Practice*

Mississippi Choctaw dance troupes are community-based and are normally composed entirely of members of a single community. There are seven Choctaw communities in Mississippi: Pearl River, Tucker, and Bogue Chitto in Neshoba County; Red Water and Standing Pine in Leake County; Conehatta in Newton County; and Bogue Homa in Jones County. Not all of these communities can field a dance troupe, however. The best troupes generally come from Bogue Chitto and Conehatta. Such a troupe is customarily made up of sixteen to twenty-two people, about equally divided between males and females, since most Choctaw dances require the dancers to form male-female pairs. One of the older men is the singer for the troupe.

Generally dance troupes are composed of a number of family groups. A married couple and their children will all be members of the same troupe, together with a number of other families. All of the families in the troupe are usually related by either blood or marriage, or at the very least are close friends of the other families in the troupe. Generally the older members take responsibility for initiating rehearsals, such as the one we attended in 1965. At such a rehearsal the older, more experienced dancers teach the children. There are occasional exceptions to this pattern, however. On the evening of July 18, 1974, a group composed entirely of teenagers performed before the grandstand at the Choctaw Fair. Even the singer for this group was a teenager, Tommy Denison of Conehatta community, a recent high school graduate.

When performing for the public, as at the Choctaw Fair, each group supplies its own announcer, who gives the name of the dance in English and in Choctaw and provides a short explanation, in English, of its significance. A troupe usually marches

onto the dance ground, or into the building where it is to perform, in good order and leaves in the same manner. At the 1974
Choctaw Fair the afternoon performances of Choctaw dances
were held in the Pearl River Community Facility Building, and
the Bogue Chitto dance troupe was featured. Prentis Jackson,
the leader and singer for the group, led the troupe into the large
room while beating a native-made snare drum. The drum was
put aside once the dancers had taken the floor, whereupon Jackson took up a pair of claves or striking sticks about a foot long,
which he used as rhythmic accompaniment for the dances.
After performing a series of native Choctaw dances, the group
exited, again marching slowly to the beat of the snare drum
played by Jackson.

The troupe returned a few minutes later to perform three
sets of what are called "house dances," the Choctaw version
of the French quadrille or the Anglo-American square dance.
These were accompanied by a violin. Jackson, as "caller" for
the house dances, did not actually shout or call the names
of the various figures, seven to a set, but merely whooped
"Weeeheea!" to signal the change from one to another. The
dancers, through long familiarity, knew exactly which figure in
the sequence to perform next in each set, each of which was
different, and no dancer showed the slightest hesitation in his or
her movements.

The outside performances before the grandstand each evening of the fair by other Mississippi Choctaw dance troupes
were similar, but they lacked the snare drum entry and exit and
the sequence of house dance sets at the end. It was obvious that
the various community dance troupes were competing with
each other to see which could field the best troupe, and each
had its group of supporters from the home community.

A visitor to the Mississippi Choctaw Fair who is familiar
with Indian gatherings in Oklahoma or elsewhere in the Plains
states immediately senses a different atmosphere in Mississippi.
For example, one searches in vain for the powwow camping
area where participants and their families sleep, cook and eat,
and socialize with the locals and other visitors between dance
performances. Instead, the singers and dancers from each community arrive as a group, perform their sequence of dances, and

then return to their home community in the evening. There is no intertribal dancing, and the members of one community dance troupe never join in the performances of other troupes. Likewise, the dancers march onto the dance floor or dancing area as community groups rather than entering in ones or twos, powwow style.

Although this pattern reminds one very strongly of the non-Indian world, where nightclub or theatrical entertainers keep pretty much to themselves after performing their individual "acts" or "numbers," it is probably an old Choctaw pattern reflecting intracommunity solidarity rather than a product of white acculturation. Blanchard, in his study of Mississippi Choctaw sports (1981) reports the same pattern in this sector of Choctaw culture. He notes that basketball (p. 79) and softball (p. 81) teams tend to be community-based and, writing of the baseball games popular in the 1940s and 1950s, he comments: "The intracommunal aspects of the events are viewed as more important than the broader intergroup dimension. . . . Parents have guarded against social intercourse among the children of the different communities represented and have limited their own interaction with members of other communities. In fact, it is said that at the classic picnics of the '40s and '50s, visiting groups would normally participate only in the affairs surrounding their own scheduled baseball contests, departing soon after they had been eliminated from the tournament" (Blanchard 1981:126).

This same feeling of community as opposed to tribal or Pan-Indian identity is also evident, though to a much lesser degree, among the Creeks and Seminoles in Oklahoma, formerly neighbors of the Choctaws in the Southeast. Here the members of one tribal town generally arrive at a Stomp Dance or Green Corn Ceremony as a group and lend their primary support to their own town's Stomp leaders. With these Muskhogeans, however, the feeling of intracommunity solidarity does not preclude participation in dance episodes led by members of other towns. Except for the sacred "daytime" dances of the Green Corn Ceremony, in which participation is strictly limited to members of the local town, Creek and Seminole dances are open to all present who wish to participate.

The foregoing should not be interpreted as standoffishness on the part of the Choctaws. In both Mississippi and Oklahoma, Choctaws are a most hospitable people. Plains Indian and white visitors to the Mississippi Choctaw Fair are often invited to come and dine or even to stay overnight at individual Choctaw homes and are proudly shown the local landmarks by enthusiastic Choctaw guides. Likewise, at rehearsals or performances *in the local community* in both Mississippi and Oklahoma, visitors are entertained royally and invited to join the various dances.

Musical Instruments

Five musical instruments are used in native contexts by present-day Choctaws: claves or striking sticks, a drum of aboriginal type, a drum copied after the Euro-American snare drum, sleigh bells or other small bells, and a cane flute of a characteristic type. Gourd rattles, mentioned in historical sources, are now totally obsolete. Claves are the characteristic accompaniment to dance songs among the Mississippi Choctaws and are also used by Eugene Wilson's Oklahoma Choctaw dance troupe, whose music and dance tradition is entirely derived from that of the Mississippi groups. Claves were formerly used to accompany dance songs by the now-extinct Bayou Lacomb Choctaw band in Louisiana. A drum of aboriginal type is now used to accompany dance songs by only one Choctaw group, Buster Ned's Sixtown troupe in Oklahoma, though use of drums seems to have been general at an earlier period. A type of drum copied after the whites' snare drum is a standard artifact among the Mississippi Choctaws. It is not, however, used to accompany dance songs, but is employed only in processions and to "drum up enthusiasm" in connection with the stickball game. Strings and loops of sleigh bells and/or hawk bells are worn as costume accessories by some of the male dancers in Buster Ned's troupe. They provide a jingling accent to the movements of the dancers. Such bells were also worn, until a few years ago, by some Mississippi Choctaw male dancers and are mentioned for the Bayou Lacomb Choctaws as well. A single sleigh bell, held in the hand, is also used by the singer for Buster Ned's troupe to beat time for a part of one dance. The cane end flute or whistle is not used in connection with dances but rather for conjuring in connection with the stickball game. It is apparently obsolescent and is limited to the Mississippi Choctaws. Gourd rattles, long obsolete, were carried in the hand by male dancers in the early historic period.

Claves or Striking Sticks (Tipiⁿha)

Claves or striking sticks are the most salient musical instrument of the Mississippi Choctaws at the present time. They are simply two billets of hard, resonant wood about fourteen inches (35 cm) in length, squared at the grip for about six inches (15 cm) and left round at the striking end. The singer or "chanter," as he is sometimes called in Mississippi, strikes the right-hand stick on the top of the left-hand one, near its end, to provide the rhythmic accompaniment to certain songs. In performances I observed, Mississippi Choctaw singers used claves to accompany the Doublehead, Drunken-man, Jump or Stomp, Quail, Raccoon, Wedding, Tick, Turtle, and War dances. Claves were *not* used in connection with the Duck, Snake, Starting, and Stealing Partners dances, for which the human voice alone is employed.

Densmore describes the claves used by the Mississippi Choctaws during the period of her fieldwork (1933): "The only instrument used by the Mississippi Choctaw in accompanying their songs is a pair of striking sticks. These are made when needed, and those made by Sidney Wesley were about 10 inches long. The sticks are not round, but slightly flattened on two sides, affording suitable surfaces for striking together. This form of percussion is not common among the Indians but was noted among the Menominee in connection with 'magic power.'" [Densmore 1943:117]

Bushnell (1909:22) also found the instrument among the Bayou Lacomb Choctaws, writing: "During the dances one man acted as leader. He held two short sticks, hitting one on the other to keep time for the singing." Curiously, Bushnell apparently did not regard the striking sticks as a bona fide musical instrument, for in the next sentence he opines, "The only musical instrument known to the Choctaw of Bayou Lacomb is the drum." (Bushnell 1909:22).

Claves, as Densmore noted, are not a common musical instrument in North America, and it is interesting to find them elevated to the number one position among the Mississippi Choctaws. So far as I am aware they are not used by the Creeks, Seminoles, Yuchis, or Cherokees. They are, however, found here and there in eastern North America. The Tutelos use them in a funeral ceremony (Speck 1942:26, fig. 2; Kurath 1981:28), as do the Mohawks, Oneidas, Onondagas, Cayugas, and Senecas of Ontario, Quebec, and New York (Speck 1955:77). The Oklahoma Seneca-Cayugas use them, together with a drum, as accompaniment for their "Sun" or War Dance (Howard 1961: 25–26). Claves were formerly used by the Shawnees (Howard 1981:46–47), Ojibwas (Tanner 1830:350–60), and Menominees (Densmore 1932:60–61) in ceremonies designed to call game magically.

Buster Ned's troupe in Oklahoma does not use claves, employing instead a native drum to accompany those dances for which their Mississippi kinsmen use striking sticks (Double Head, Drunken-man, Jump or Stomp, Tick, and War dances) as well as for the Duck, Snake, and Stealing Partners dances, for which in Mississippi there is no instrumental accompaniment. Mississippi Choctaws who saw Ned's group perform at the Mississippi Choctaw Fair attributed this preference for the drum to the influence of Plains Indians on the Oklahomans. Ned, however, insists that his group is the more traditional in its choice of instruments.

Possibly claves came into Choctaw culture, or came to be emphasized by Mississippi and Louisiana Choctaws, as a result of a prohibition of native drums by blacks and other nonwhites in the antebellum era in the Old South because of their use as signaling devices in slave revolts.

Drums (Atepa, Atepa Bali, Atepa She Boli)

Buster Ned's contention that a drum, rather than claves, is the traditional accompaniment for Choctaw dance songs is backed up by Cushman:

> Their musical genius in the invention of musical instruments never extended beyond that of a cane flute and a small drum, which was constructed from a section cut from a small hollow tree, over the hollow part of which was stretched a fresh deer skin, cleansed from hair, which became very tight when dried,

and when struck by a stick made a dull sound, little inferior to that of our common snare drum, which could be heard at a considerable distance. . . . In all their dances they invariably danced to the sound of the indispensable drum, accompanied with the low hum of the drummer, keeping exact step with its monotonus tone. [1962:155–56]

Swanton (1931:224) speaks of this same type of Choctaw drum, noting that "cypress knees were also commonly used for the body of the drum. The opening was usually closed with a deerskin but a bearskin is said to have been employed at times."

The drum used by Adam Sampson, Bienum Pickens, and other singers for Buster Ned's troupe at the present time is about 19¹¹⁄₁₆ inches (50 cm) in diameter and 7¾ inches (20 cm) in depth. It has two skin heads laced on either side of a bent wood shell (see chapter 3, illustrations 2 and 4) or a fiberglass shell (see chapter 3, illustration 7). It is struck with a single drumstick about 19½ inches (50 cm) in length, one end of which is padded to protect the drumhead. In my opinion the form of this latter-day drum, though not the manner in which it is used, does show Plains Indian influence. These drums are made for the Choctaw-Chickasaw Heritage Committee by Buster Ned.

Another type of native-style drum was made by the Bayou Lacomb Choctaws. Bushnell pictures this drum in his short monograph and describes it as follows:

The only musical instrument known to the Choctaw of Bayou Lacomb is the drum (*the'ba*). . . . This is 30 inches in height and 15 inches in diameter. It is made of a section of black gum tree; the cylinder wall is less than 2 inches in thickness. The head consists of a piece of untanned goat skin. The skin is stretched over the open end, while wet and pliable, and is passed around a hoop made of hickory about half an inch thick. A similar hoop is placed above the first. To the second hoop are attached four narrow strips of rawhide, each of which is fastened to a peg passing diagonally through the wall of the drum. To tighten the head of the drum it is necessary merely to drive the peg farther in. In this respect, as well as in general form, the drum resembles a specimen from Virginia in the British Museum, as well as the drum even now used on the west coast of Africa. It is not possible to say whether this instrument is a purely American form or whether it shows the influence of the negro.

Unfortunately Bushnell does not indicate anywhere in his monograph when or how this drum was used, or whether it was played with one stick or two or merely slapped with the hands. His account would indicate that it was not used to accompany dance songs, for he indicates that claves were used for this purpose (Bushnell 1909:22). The drum may have been a type formerly beaten in connection with the stickball game, which was obsolete among the Bayou Lacomb Choctaws at the time of Bushnell's visit (Bushnell 1909:20). In this case certain features of its somewhat anomalous form can be explained by reference to the Choctaw snare drum, described below.

Snare Drum

I prefer to discuss this type of drum separately from those above since in both form and function it is clearly distinct and just as clearly represents an item borrowed by the Choctaws from white culture. The snare drum is at present used only by the Mississippi Choctaws. My consultant, the late Bob Henry of Bogue Chitto community, made snare drums. According to Henry, all Choctaw snare drums are copied from an original either given to the Choctaws by or captured from European soldiers in the period of the French and Indian Wars "200 or more years ago." Henry showed me, in 1965, the shell of this original snare drum, preserved by the Mississippi Choctaws as a historic relic and model. It was made of brass, with a wooden hoop at either end for tightening the heads.

The Mississippi Choctaws use the snare drum in two ways. The first is in processions, as when a troupe of dancers marches into the dance hall or onto the field where it is to perform, and likewise when it marches off. A team of stickball players also marches on and off the field led by a drummer (cf. Blanchard 1981: plate 17). The drum is also used by a stickball team's medicine man to "conjure" for his team, to "drum up enthusiasm," and to signal the progress of the game. Thus Densmore writes: "Each medicine man at a ball game carried a drum, beating upon it during the game. Robert Henry, Sidney Wesley, and

Gus Willis said that, within their knowledge, the drum has been used at no other time by the Mississippi Choctaw" (1943:117).

Densmore apparently did not recognize that this type of drum was not a native form, for in her next sentence she writes: "Evidently this was in general use at an earlier time . . ." (1943:117).

Swanton also failed to recognize the snare drum as a borrowing from white culture, for he gives the following account of it from his informant Simpson Tubby with no comment:

> He said it was made of a section of black gum or tupelo gum, hollowed out and 12 or 16 inches across, and of about the same length. Over the ends of this deerskins were fitted, each skin being first brought over the outside of a hoop or "cuff" and fastened tight, the cuff being just large enough to fit over the end of the body. After these had been put in place, a larger cuff was made and fitted tight over each and the two outside cuffs were fastened together by means of diagonal cords. Midway of the drum were two other cuffs or hoops fastened to the diagonal cords in such a way that when they were pushed in opposite directions they tightened the heads of the drum. The cuffs were made of white switch hickory, the cords anciently of deer hide, but later of store leather. Two deer-hide strings were allowed to lie across the end of the drum opposite that which was struck. One of these was looser than the other, so that two distinct notes resulted.
>
> Drumsticks were made principally of maple, poplar, or ash. Each had a knob at the end, one made smaller to "beat the seconds," while most of the noise was made with the other. They beat on the end of the drum opposite that across which the strings lay but most of the noise is supposed to have been made by the other end, the compressed air transferring the vibrations across. If they wished to protect the drumhead they wrapped the knobs of the drumsticks with cloth. [Swanton 1931:224]

The details of construction given by Tubby, plus the mention of the use of two sticks in connection with this drum, clearly identify it as the snare drum, made by Choctaws using native materials.

Blanchard, in his study of Mississippi Choctaw sports, repeatedly mentions the snare drum. The "processional" use of

the drum is noted thus: "Prior to each game, the two teams assemble near the tribal offices, some 200 yards from the playing
field. From here they parade to the ball field in a single file, as a
drummer leads the way, ceremoniously pounding a small, commercially made drum in a slow but steady rhythm" (1981:67).
Of its use during the game he writes: "The contemporary racket
game is marked by the presence of a degree of traditional ritual.
Not only does the event reflect many specifically Choctaw
norms and values, but ritual personnel are also involved either
directly or indirectly. The only visible role is that of the drummer, who, by virtue of the steady, rhythmic pounding of his instrument, brings a certain order to the hodgepodge of activities
characterizing the game" (Blanchard 1981:70–71). Elsewhere
he quotes his informant Baxter York as to the function of the
drum: "Before the stickball game, the drum would begin to
beat, and you would know they were going to have a game
somewhere. . . . Drums were used to pep up the game and add
excitement. They beat them with a certain rhythm. This would
change when one of the teams scored. This way the message
could be sent to people in surrounding areas. They could tell by
the beat of the drum that one of the teams had scored a point"
(quoted in Blanchard 1981:35).

Like Swanton and Densmore before him, however,
Blanchard did not realize that the Mississippi Choctaw drum is
merely a homemade version of the European snare drum. Thus
on page 67 of his book he refers to it as a "small, commercially
made drum," but on pages 35–36 he implies an aboriginal origin for the drum used during the ball game: "Using a percussion
instrument made by stretching a deerskin over a tree trunk,
earthen pot, or kettle, the drummer beat no predetermined pattern but simply kept pace with the ball game" (Blanchard 1981).

In addition to the way it is made and played, the occasions when the snare drum is used by the Mississippi Choctaws clearly identify its alien origin. It is *not* used to accompany
dance songs but, as with military snare drums, to provide accompaniment for marches and processions, and to advertise
and announce the fortunes of stickball teams. In short, the
Choctaws have preserved the use of the snare drum in much
the way it was employed by whites in the Old South—in military parades and to draw a crowd for a show or an auction (in-

cluding slave auctions). In reference to the latter function one recalls the term *drummer* as applied to a commercial traveler in U.S. English.

Despite its non-Indian origin, the snare drum has become fully integrated into Mississippi Choctaw culture. Such drums are prized possessions of their owners and are rarely sold to non-Indians. At the Mississippi Choctaw Fair the various communities often display their native-made snare drums, along with other handicrafts, in the exhibit building. Until a few years ago, according to my informant, the late Bob Henry of Bogue Chitto, there were even drum-beating contests at the fair, the drummers from the various communities vying with one another for the title "best Choctaw drummer."

Though at present the snare drum is most visible among the Mississippi Choctaws, it was adopted by other southeastern tribes as well, and is still used by one of them, the Yuchis. Thus in 1761, Timberlake observed that the Cherokees he encountered used not only their native drums but also some military snare drums they had captured from the English after the massacre at Fort Loudon (Timberlake 1948:63). The Creeks also remember that they secured snare drums, together with flags, medals, and silver gorgets, when they made treaties with the English (Barney Leader, personal communication, 1974). Today the Yuchis still employ a snare drum during their annual Green Corn ceremonies at their square ground near Kellyville, Oklahoma, where I observed it in use in 1969 and 1974. Like the Mississippi Choctaws, the Yuchis do not use the snare drum as accompaniment to dance songs, but rather to assemble members of the tribe to hear Busk speeches by square-ground officials. In the Southwest the snare drum was adopted from the Spaniards by a number of Pueblo groups. There again, as in the Southeast, it was used for processions and announcements, never to accompany dances.

Bells (Łale Salowa)

Sleigh bells, hawk bells, and other small bells are sometimes worn as a part of the dancing costume by Oklahoma Choctaw men and were formerly used by male dancers among the Mississippi and Louisiana Choctaws as well. Such bells have been used by Choctaw dancers since at least the early part of the eighteenth century, for the *French Relation* describes their use in the period about 1740 as follows: "When they have these dances they begin about two hours after midday. They are painted. They put on their finest clothing, and make a belt of about forty pot-metal bells as big as the fist. Others put on little bells, and if they have big bells, and are able to carry them, they take them to these dances, loving the noise extraordinarily . . ." (Swanton 1931:254–55).

Although such bells were no longer worn when Bushnell observed and photographed the Bayou Lacomb Choctaw dances, he secured a description of their former use: "When dancing, the men often wore strings of small brass bells around each leg, below the knee. These bells were highly prized by the older generation" (Bushnell 1909:11).

Among the Mississippi Choctaws, bells are obsolete today, though they continued in use into the 1960s. In 1965, Wilson Morris, of Bogue Chitto community, showed me his set of dance bells, a loop of twine about 4½ inches (11 cm) in length and 3 inches (8 cm) wide with a sleigh bell about 1¼ inches (3 cm) in diameter at the center or bottom of the loop. This large bell was flanked on either side by slightly smaller bells, and these in turn by still smaller bells, ending with very small hawk bells at the top. The spaces between the bells were heavily wrapped with cord. This loop of bells, Morris said, was worn at the dancer's side, held in place by the same ribbons which tie together the two ends of the dancer's baldrics or shoulder sashes.

Bells are still worn by some of the younger male dancers of Buster Ned's Sixtown troupe, but they are worn at the ankle. They are strings of sleigh bells, about 1¼ inches (3 cm) in diameter, riveted to a leather strap about 12 inches (30 cm) long, which is equipped with tie thongs at either end. Generally a dancer wears bells around only one ankle. Unlike Prairie and Plains Indians, the Choctaw men tie their ankle bells quite loosely, and therefore only a faint tinkling noise can be heard when the wearer dances.

One additional use of bells was noted among the Sixtown Choctaws. This is the use of a single sleigh bell, held in the hand, used to beat time by the singer in the first portion of the Duck Dance. The sound of this bell appears clearly in the

Choctaw-Chickasaw Heritage Committee's recording of this dance. During the second part of the song a drum is used as accompaniment.

Whistles or Flutes (Uskulushi)

Frances Densmore is the only source who provides detailed information regarding the construction or use of the whistle or flute by the Choctaws: "These were blown by the medicine men on the night before that [the stickball] game, and during the game to bring success to certain groups of players. No other use of the instrument was mentioned by the informants" (1943:117–18). Later in the same work we read:

> Five or six medicine men were attached to each team of players, in former times, and each medicine man had two or three whistles, a drum, and a wand with some small object at the tip. Robert Henry remembered such a wand as having what looked like a red bird at its end. Its use was not described. The whistles are still used and are of different lengths, each having a different mark on one side. . . .
>
> On the night before a ball game, the whistles are blown by the medicine men, there is "talking" in which it is stated that "You are going to win the game," and the song for success is sung. The whistles are blown during a game, and the medicine men beat on their drums, but there is no singing while the game is in progress. The sound of the whistles during a game was referred to as "the noise made by the witches." [1943:128]

On page 129, Densmore shows a snake design used on such a whistle (her fig. 3) and comments:

> The blowing of cane whistles by the medicine men before and during a ball game has been mentioned. Robert Henry has three of these whistles, which he is accustomed to use at the game, and he recorded the sound of each, playing one after another in rapid succession. Each whistle had its special marking. The first was 12½ inches in length and etched (burned) with the design shown in figure 3. The second is shown in plate 20, figure 1, and is in the possession of the United States National Museum. This and the third whistle were 11 inches in length. The third whistle was etched with Robert Henry's personal mark (fig. 4). . . . As shown in the portrait of Robert Henry blowing the whistle (pl. 20, fig. 2)

the first finger of each hand was placed over a sound hole, the middle finger of the player's left hand being placed between the two round holes. [1943:129]

In 1965 my informant, Bob Henry (the son of Robert Henry, Densmore's informant), supplied me with essentially the same information regarding the whistles as that which his father had given Densmore. On that same occasion he gave me a cane whistle of the type described. This instrument he retrieved from its hiding place beneath his house just before giving it to me. The fact that the whistle was kept *outside* the dwelling (and hence away from the women and children) probably indicates that it was regarded as a "medicine" object, endowed with supernatural power that would be diminished if it were stored in proximity to women, especially during their menstruation.

The use of whistles for conjuring at stickball games has apparently disappeared since 1965, for I did not see any in use during the stickball game at the Choctaw Fair in 1974, nor are they mentioned, except by reference to Densmore's work, in Blanchard's book on Mississippi Choctaw sports (1981).

Gourd rattles

Gourd rattles of the type common in eastern North America were used by the Choctaws in the eighteenth century but have long been obsolete. In the *French Relation* the writer, describing male dancers, observed: "They carry a rattle (chichiquoia) in the hand, or a war club, or a pistol" (Swanton 1931:255).

Costume

When participating in public performances of Choctaw dances, today's Choctaws wear their national costume. This costume, for both sexes, is quite distinctive and readily distinguishes the wearer as a Choctaw rather than a member of some other southeastern tribe. There are only slight differences between the Mississippi and Oklahoma Choctaws in terms of dress. Most of the items making up both the man's and the woman's costume are derived from the clothing styles of southern whites in the nineteenth century. Certain of the component parts, however, are made and decorated in a distinctive Choctaw manner, and both the male and female ensembles are now so well integrated into Choctaw culture that they constitute a tribal badge.

The costume of the men and boys, from head to toe, consists of the following eight items:

1. A low-crowned black felt hat (*shapo*) is usually decorated with a band made of two commercial rayon ribbons. Often there is a tiny ribbon bow at the front of the band, and the ends of the ribbons are allowed to hang loose over the brim of the hat for several inches in back. The name of the hat in Choctaw, *shapo,* derives from the French *chapeau* and indicates the European group from which the Choctaws secured their headgear. According to Claude Medford, Jr., the older Cajun men of Louisiana often wear a hat identical to that used by the Choctaws. Medford reports that until recently both Choctaws and French-speaking Louisianans ordered these hats from suppliers in France.

Sometimes older Choctaw men wear an eagle feather at one side of the hat, or even one on each side. I have also seen men wearing a colored turkey or goose feather that has had most of the rachis shaved away so that the web vibrates rapidly in the slightest breeze. This is an old southeastern Indian trait, and I have observed feathers treated in this manner among the Creeks, Seminoles, and Yuchis in Oklahoma as well. Formerly some men wore silver headbands or crowns as hatbands. These were the same pierced silver headbands formerly worn in connection with the cloth turban, which was the male head covering antedating the felt hat.

2. The traditional Choctaw shirt (*ilefoka lomba*) is collarless and buttons at the back of the neck. These shirts are invariably in a solid color of cotton, usually red, blue, yellow, white, or pink, with a decoration of finely cut and stitched appliqué work in a contrasting color on the front and arms. The designs employed in Choctaw appliqué work have names and a symbolic meaning. They will be discussed later in this section.

3. Around the neck some men wear a bright silk scarf (*natpaski*), an openwork beaded necklace (*shikalla nondzhi*), or sim-

ply several strands of large beads strung in loops. I have also
seen Plains-style beaded bolo ties and choker necklaces, or
simply a commercially made silk cravat.

4. An optional item worn over the shirt is the beaded cloth
shoulder belt or baldric (*skikalla εskofatshi*). It is of a color that
contrasts with the color of the shirt and is beautifully beaded in
traditional Choctaw motifs. Today only a few of the men and
boys, usually older men, wear these baldrics, but old photographs and costume dolls indicate that their use was once more
general. One old photograph taken in 1907 even shows a young
girl wearing a pair of baldrics, but this certainly was never common practice. Usually baldrics are made and worn in matching
sets, but that is not invariably the case. Baldrics were once worn
by Creeks, Seminoles, Yuchis, Cherokees, and even Shawnees,
but they are now seen only among the Choctaws. I was told
that at one time each Choctaw community had its characteristic designs.

5. Another optional item is the beaded belt (*εskofatshi*). It
may be decorated in the same designs and beadwork tech-
niques as the baldric (item 4, above), but I have also seen recent
examples done in loomwork using Pan-Indian geometric designs. Beaded belts are purely ornamental and are worn over the
ordinary leather belt used to hold up the trousers.

6. Fastened to the belt on one side, either right or left, is a
bunch of long ribbons of various colors (*sita lapushki*) which
may hang nearly to the ground. These ribbons may be a survival of the ends of the finger-woven yarn sash formerly worn
by Choctaw men. Trailing behind the moving dancers, the ribbons provide an interesting accent to their movements.

7. Trousers or slacks (*obala foka*) in Mississippi are usually
black. The male dancers in Eugene Wilson's Oklahoma troupe,
however, were completely outfitted in white slacks when I saw
them perform in 1974. Male dancers in Buster Ned's Sixtown
troupe often have a stripe of appliqué on the outer side of each
trouser leg, and three of the younger men in his group have
shirts and trousers of the same matching color and appliqué
design.

8. Ordinary commercially made shoes or moccasins (*shul-
ush,* from the English word *shoes*) complete the present-day
male dancer's costume. Historic Choctaw dolls indicate that un-

til 1860 or 1870 Choctaw men and women wore soft-soled moccasins of native manufacture. These were of the classical southeastern type, puckered to a single seam at the top of the foot and with large ankle flaps.

Bells (*ṭale saḷowa*), as noted earlier, are still worn by some of the male dancers in Buster Ned's troupe and were formerly worn by male dancers in Mississippi and Louisiana.

The hunting coat (*na foka paḷafa,* lit. "split garment") is an obsolete item of male costume. It appears in photographs of Choctaw men taken in 1907 and 1909 and in the Catlin paintings. The coat was worn over the shirt and was decorated with appliqué designs at the cuffs, front opening, and hem. Such hunting coats were widespread in the Southeast in the nineteenth century and the first few decades of the twentieth. They survived until the late 1960s among the Creeks, Seminoles, and Yuchis in Oklahoma but apparently went out of use somewhat earlier among the Choctaws.

Silver armbands (*shakba ɛlhfoa*), silver gorgets, and face paint (*tishi humma*) are also items of male adornment no longer seen but still remembered.

The women and girls wear a costume composed of the following six items:

1. The comb (*issɛp isht ɛlpi*) is usually made of silver with fancy cutout work, but in Densmore's days it was sometimes made of an old-fashioned man's celluloid collar (cf. Densmore 1943:116). The comb is worn just back of the crown of the head.

2. A bead necklace (*shikalla nondzhi*) is similar to that of the men, done in "net" or openwork beadwork, like a small bib in its shape.

3. The traditional Choctaw woman's dress (*Chaata hoyo ilifoka*) is the Choctaw version of a common style worn by white women in the early nineteenth century. It has full sleeves, either full length or three-quarters length, a fitted top, and a long skirt with one (Oklahoma) or two (Mississippi) ruffles at the bottom. Like the man's shirt, the woman's dress is of a solid color such as red, blue, yellow, pink, or light green, and it is ornamented with cutout appliqué work in a contrasting color on the bosom, back, cuffs, and in two or three rows at and just above the hem.

4. Over the dress is worn a long white apron (*na foka in-*

tikpa takali) with ruffles at the bottom and sides and with long ties in the back. Sometimes the apron is decorated with a single row of appliqué at the edge in a contrasting color.

5. Some women and girls wear a bunch of long ribbons (*sita lapushki*) of various colors hanging from the back of the neck nearly to the hem of the skirt.

6. Commercially made shoes or moccasins (*shalush*) complete the woman's costume.

A variety of hair styles is seen. In Mississippi mature women generally wear their hair brushed back from the forehead and tied or fastened with a comb at the back of the neck, while younger women and girls wear theirs parted in the middle and falling loose over the shoulders. In Oklahoma one is more likely to see shorter hair and permanent waves. Two braids are sometimes worn by younger women and girls in both states, probably a reflection of Pan-Indian sentiments. In both Mississippi and Oklahoma younger girls sometimes wear Pan-Indian–style beaded headbands and beaded "powwow princess" coronets.

Silver earrings, bracelets, and finger rings are seen in both Mississippi and Oklahoma.

Obsolete items of feminine costume are face paint (*tishi humma*) and a second silver comb worn at the front of the head to "frame the face." Shawls also appear as items of female costume in photographs taken in 1907.

Perhaps the most characteristic feature of present-day Choctaw costuming, both male and female, is the cutout appliqué work noted above in connection with the men's shirts and the women's dresses and aprons. There seem to be a limited number of designs employed in this type of ornamentation. Buster Ned supplied the following interpretation of some of these appliqué designs:

1. The diamond design, ⟡⟡, is derived from the markings of a diamondback rattlesnake. This design appears on two of the women's dresses and on the men's shirts in illustration 2 (see chapter 3).

2. The Saint Andrew's cross design, ✕, according to Buster Ned, derives from the Choctaw stickball game (*kabutsha*): "In years past [the player] when the game was over . . . would hang the sticks on the walls of the house, and put [them] in the

shape of an **X**. This design means 'May our paths cross again and again.'" The design appears on the woman's dress and on the sleeves of the man's shirt in illustration 4 (see chapter 3). The Saint Andrew's cross design is also commonly seen in beadwork.

3. The half-diamond design, △ or ^∨^ , according to Buster Ned, "is derived from [the] life of the people. The Choctaw people believed in the Great Spirit (God) in that their life followed an imaginary road (shown in sketch above). [The design symbolizes] that when they give aid to someone sick, they come off this imaginary road, and when the sick was well, he returned to this road and continued. [Likewise] when he did something bad, he again left this road, only he was on the opposite side, thus the half diamond design."

4. The road design, ▭ , according to Buster Ned, represents the "road of life" which one travels in his or her span on earth, as mentioned in connection with the half-diamond design above. It is almost always used in connection with another design, as on the woman's dress in illustration 4 (see chapter 3).

5. The circle design, ○, represents the Choctaw tribe. Buster Ned comments: "The Choctaws believed, and still do, that we live in a circle (imaginary) and that, in this circle, a man or woman cannot talk about (gossip) or tell bad tales on another Choctaw. If this happens then this is . . . passed on until [within] a short period of time the person who did the talking finds himself or herself being shunned by his fellow tribesmen and he is then 'out of the circle' and he'll be wondering why."

6. The ball design, ◉ , represents the ball used in the Choctaw stickball game. According to Buster this design was worn only on the garments of the male stickball players. This design is apparently obsolete, as I have never seen it in use in either Mississippi or Oklahoma. It is nevertheless clearly identifiable as a representation of the Choctaw stickball game ball. The ball used by the Choctaws is neatly covered with interwoven rawhide or leather strips, which explains the interior linework in this design.

Certain other Choctaw designs are seen only in beadwork and never in appliqué. The most famous and characteristic of these is

7. The reversed spiral or "coiled snake" design, ◎◎. This

design represents the giant horned serpent of southeastern my-
thology coiling and uncoiling. It is definitely prehistoric in origin, as it appears as a pottery design on vessels from the Mississippian archaeological culture. In the eighteenth and nineteenth
centuries it was in widespread use as a beadwork design on baldrics. I have observed it on baldrics collected from the Cherokees, Creeks, Alabamas, and Coushattas as well as from the
Choctaws. At present it continues in use only among the Choctaws. The coiled snake appears in the baldrics worn by men in
illustrations 2, 4, and 6 (see chapter 3). In 1965 I collected a baldric from Wilson Morris, of Bogue Chitto community in Mississippi, which employs the reversed spiral motif together with
design 2, the Saint Andrew's cross. The reversed spiral design is
sometimes split into two parts or otherwise modified.

    8. Another common beadwork design is the ⬦, identi-
fied by Wilson Morris as the "friendship" design.

    9. The sunburst and sunburst enclosing a star are also com-
mon beadwork designs, but I did not secure any interpretations
of their symbolism.

3. The Dances

Choctaw dances, at least all of those that have survived to the present day, are easy to perform and require little special expertise. Any able-bodied person who can both walk and keep time has no difficulty joining in and performing the dances even if he or she has never seen them before. The dances are mostly slow to medium in tempo and therefore not particularly exciting for spectators. They were clearly developed mainly for the enjoyment of the participants, and all but three (Duck Dance, Quail Dance, and War Dance) involve at least some of the dancers joining in with or responding to the songs of the principal singer.

All surviving Choctaw dances are open to members of both sexes. In the past there was at least one dance, the Eagle Dance (Catlin 1844, II:127), that was limited to men only, but today even the Choctaw War Dance involves female partici-pants, a fact the Choctaws are quick to point out to visitors from other tribes. The male role, however, is emphasized in this dance, which is accompanied by a solo male singer. In three other dances (Double Head Dance, Jump or Stomp Dance, and Starting Dance) only the male dancers respond to the songs of the principal singer in antiphonal fashion, indicating that in times past these four dances may have been limited to males, or at least considered primarily the province of the men. All of the other dances are equally balanced between the two sexes. In seven (Drunken-man, Raccoon, Snake, Wedding, Stealing Part-ners, Tick, and Turtle dances) both men and women join in with the principal singer, while in two more (Duck Dance and Quail Dance), though a solo male singer provides the musical accompaniment the two sexes are balanced with each other in the choreography.

Descriptions of each of the surviving Choctaw dances follow. When names of the dances or details of performance differ
from one community or area to another, these differences are
noted. Likewise, after each description from my own observations I have included comparative material from Bushnell's
(1909) descriptions of the Bayou Lacomb (Louisiana) Choctaw
dances and Densmore's (1943) descriptions of Mississippi Choctaw dances observed in 1933, plus any additional comparative
data I have been able to turn up.

Starting Dance

Members of other southeastern tribes, such as the Creeks,
Seminoles, and Cherokees, and non-Indians who are somewhat
familiar with southeastern American Indian music and dance
often ask, when the subject of Choctaw dances comes up, "Do
the Choctaws have a dance like the Stomp Dance?" The Choctaws of course have many dances with antiphonal leader-chorus
responses, and sometimes their Jump Dance is called "Stomp
Dance" in English. The Choctaw dance that is most like the
Creek and Seminole *Opanka haco,* or Ordinary Stomp Dance, or
the dance known to the Cherokees as *Dilsti* is the Starting
Dance. It is odd that this dance, which is so popular among the
Creeks, Seminoles, Yuchis, Cherokees, and other southeastern
tribes that it overshadows all others, is obsolescent among the
Choctaws in both Mississippi and Oklahoma. In fact I have
seen the dance performed only once, by a group of dancers
from Bogue Chitto community who were rehearsing for the
1965 Choctaw Fair. The dance was performed twice on that occasion. Prentis Jackson and Ida May Frazer were the leaders of
one set, Henry and Ovie Joe of another.

A long double file of dancers, men on the outside, women
on the inside, move in a counterclockwise circular progression
employing a trotting step. The leader, a man, sings out a short
phrase which is answered in antiphonal fashion by the men
and boys behind him. He then sings another phrase, and so on.
Except for the fact that the women dance in a separate file from
the men, and that no leg rattles are employed by the women,
the dance is identical in choreography, and very similar musically, to the "Ordinary Stomp Dance" of Oklahoma. According

to Prentis Jackson, the Starting Dance is rarely performed today. In earlier times it was used to initiate a night of social dancing.

Jump Dance or Stomp Dance (*Tolubli Hila*)

The Jump Dance begins with the dancers formed in a single line, the male members of the troupe at the head, the women and girls at the rear. Each dancer (except for the leader) has his or her right arm linked to the left arm of the person directly in front, and each faces slightly inward, that is, to the left or center of the circle. The singer, using claves (Mississippi Choctaws) or a hand drum (Oklahoma Sixtown Choctaws), stands to one side of the dancers. He begins the dance with a series of short cries, which are answered in antiphonal fashion by the male members of the group but not by the women dancers. The dancers employ a slow toe-heel left, toe-heel right step during this first or introductory portion of the dance, moving in a counterclockwise direction behind the leader. The leader gradually forms the group into a large ring.

On musical cue the entire line of dancers turns so that the dancers now face the center of the dance area and, arms still linked, they begin a heavy hopping step. In some dance troupes this hopping is done on alternate feet: left, right, left, and so on. In other troupes the hopping is on both feet simultaneously. In either case the hopping is done in strict time to the beat of the claves or the drum. As they hop, the group slowly progresses in a counterclockwise direction. The male dancers generally emit sharp yells at the beginning of this "stomping" episode. Sometimes, if there are a number of small children dancing, they form their own ring, separate from that of the adults.

In their 1974 performances Eugene Wilson's troupe started the Jump Dance with the sexes alternating—first the leader (a man), then a woman, then a man, and so on—but otherwise the dance was performed as described above.

A variant form of the dance, though called by the same name in both English and Choctaw, was observed at Bogue Chitto community in 1965. On that occasion the dance began with the sexes alternating, as above, but when the "jumping" began, they formed into couples, men and women facing each other. The women were inside the ring, the men outside, the

Illustration 1. Jump Dance at the Choctaw Fair, Pearl River,
Mississippi, 1974. (*Photograph by James Howard*)

men facing inward and the women out. In this position both
groups hopped on both feet, moving in a counterclockwise direction. Another dance, identical in its choreography, followed
the Jump Dance on this occasion. It was identified as the Borrow Money Dance by Prentis Jackson.

The narrator for a performance of the Jump Dance by the
Bogue Chitto troupe at the Mississippi Choctaw Fair in 1974
noted that the dance was performed in celebration of victories
in war by the Choctaws in ancient times, while the narrator for
Eugene Wilson's Choctaw dancers said that the Jump Dance
was the principal "good time" dance of the old-time Choctaws
and was often danced after a successful hunt. Both statements
are probably accurate. Bob Henry, my Bogue Chitto informant,
said that the Jump Dance is sometimes called the Link Arms
Dance because of this characteristic feature of its performance.

The antiphonal music of the Choctaw Jump or Stomp
Dance, particularly its use of short musical cries or shouts at the
beginning followed by longer antiphonal phrases, bears a close
resemblance to the music of the so-called Stomp Dance (*Opanka
Haco*) of the Creeks and Seminoles, but it is completely different
in its choreography.

Although Bushnell does not describe any dance called either Jump Dance or Stomp Dance for the Bayou Lacomb Choctaws, it is very likely that this is the same as his *Nanena Hitkla*

or Man Dance: "All lock arms and form a ring; all sing and the ring revolves rapidly. No one remains in the ring" (Bushnell 1909:20). The fact that only men answer the leader in this dance may have led to its being called the Man Dance by the Bayou Lacomb group.

Densmore saw the dance performed at Pearl River community in Mississippi in 1933:

> On the occasion of the writer's visit, the Stomp dance was given by request, following the other dances. Men and women stood in a circle, facing the center. They were not in couples but in any desired order, and all joined in the songs. The leader of the singing was an old man, who stood in the middle of the circle. As stated, the leader of the singing need not take part in the dancing, though a young man usually leads the line of dancers and sings. The motion of the dance consisted in jumping with both feet at once, the circle of dancers moving in a contra clockwise direction. No instrumental accompaniment was used with these songs. [1943:160]

Note that Densmore indicates that both men and women joined in the singing and that no instrumental accompaniment was used. These features are in contrast to my own observations of the dance in both Mississippi and Oklahoma. Densmore recorded and analyzed twelve Stomp Dance songs (1943:161–71). She gives *Hila Tolupli* as the name of the dance (p. 143), which is nearly identical to the term I found in both Mississippi and Oklahoma.

Borrow-Money Dance

I have seen this dance only once, at the rehearsal of the Bogue Chitto community dance troupe on July 25, 1965. My notes say that it is identical with the Stomp or Jump Dance in its choreography. I did not obtain a native name for it.

Double Header or Backward-and-Forward Dance (*Hila Falama*)

At the beginning of this dance the dancers, men and women alternating, are arranged in a single file. All link arms and, when the music begins, walk slowly in a counterclockwise direction. On musical cue all turn ninety degrees to the left and begin jumping in time to the music, first on the left foot, then on the right, then on the left again, the entire group still moving in a counterclockwise progression. After a short while they reverse, moving clockwise, and after a while reverse again to a counter-clockwise direction. Except for the change in directions, the choreography of this dance is identical to that of the Jump or Stomp Dance.

The music of the dance is antiphonal. The singer, always a man, begins the dance with a series of short cries, which are answered by the male members of the group but not by the women. He accompanies himself with either claves (Missis-sippi Choctaw) or a hand drum (Oklahoma Choctaw).

The Sixtown Choctaws call this dance Double Head or Double Header because the person at one end of the rank leads the group to the right for a time, then the person at the other end leads them to the left, and so on. Thus there are two leaders or heads for the dance.

Bushnell gives the same Choctaw name for the dance that I collected but calls it "Dance Go-and-Come" in English. He de-scribes it thus: "All lock arms and the line moves sideways, first in one direction, then in the opposite, but never backward or forward. If there are too many dancers for a single line, addi-tional lines are formed. All taking part sing the particular song for this dance" (1909:21).

Densmore (1943:171–72) gives one song of this dance. Her informant, Sidney Wesley, termed it a "variation or change in the Stomp dance." The Choctaw name of the dance *Hila Falama* might be literally translated "Dance Returning."

Mrs. Mose Burris, wife of the famous Oklahoma Choctaw law enforcement officer, recalled that she met her husband while performing this dance: "I use to dance stomp dance. That the way I meet Burris. We dancing double head dance" (Milligan 1976:52).

Tick Dance (*Shatenni Hila*) or Walk Dance (*Tanowa Hila*)

The Tick Dance or Walk Dance is often the first and some-times the last dance in contemporary Choctaw performances.

It is very dignified and solemn and serves to show off the finery of the dancers to excellent advantage. A single file of dancers, men at the front and women at the rear, moves in a slow counterclockwise progression. In Mississippi the step is simply a slow step forward with the left foot, then a slow bringing up of the right foot beside it. Buster Ned's Sixtown troupe uses a more elaborate step consisting of a step forward with the left foot after which the right foot is brought forward and touched briefly to the ground in a position in advance of the left but then immediately pulled back to a position slightly behind the left. The dancer then shifts his or her weight to the right foot and takes another step forward with the left, and so on. In some dance troupes each dancer (except for the man at the head of the file) places his or her right hand on the shoulder of the person ahead. In other troupes the dancers link arms.

In both Mississippi and Oklahoma the dancers, both men and women, answer the lead phrase of the singer in antiphonal style. The singer keeps time with claves (Mississippi) or a hand drum (Sixtown Choctaws). The Bogue Chitto dance troupe in Mississippi often uses this dance as an exit processional when giving a public performance. In that case their singer, Prentis

Illustration 2. Tick or Walk Dance performed by the Choctaw-Chickasaw Heritage Committee near Madill, Oklahoma, 1981.
(*Photograph by James Howard*)

Jackson, taps his snare drum to beat time as the group leaves the dance area. This is the only time I have ever seen the snare drum used to accompany dancing by Mississippi Choctaws.

The Tick Dance is noted for its many songs and is undoubtedly the favorite dance of older dancers in both Mississippi and Oklahoma.

In Mississippi the preferred English name for the dance is "Walk Dance." The Oklahoma Sixtown Choctaws prefer "Tick Dance." Both names for the dance are, however, recognized in both states. I rather imagine that the name "Walk Dance" was adopted because it was considered less offensive to white audiences, just as "Goose Dance" was substituted for "Drunken-man."

Bushnell found the Tick Dance among the Bayou Lacomb Choctaws, and his description of it, though somewhat imprecise, is interesting in that it provides an explanation regarding the dance's name: "The dancers lock arms and form in straight lines. First they move forward two or three steps [*sic*], then backward, but they gradually advance. When they take the forward step they stamp with the right foot, as if crushing ticks on the ground, at the same time looking down, supposedly at the doomed insects. During the dance all sing with many repetitions the song here given, the words of which have no special meaning" (1909:20–21).

In 1933, Densmore (1943:136–43) recorded twelve Tick Dance songs, eleven of which are transcribed in her monograph. Her consultant, Sidney Wesley, described the choreography of the dance: "Men, women, and children take part in this dance and all join in the singing. Wesley said they form in a long line with the men in advance and move slowly, the step consisting in advancing the left foot, bringing the right foot to a position beside it and standing for a moment on both feet before again going forward" (Densmore 1943:135).

Stealing Partners Dance (*Itimoyabi Hila*)

This dance begins with the performers arranged in single file, the men and boys at the head of the line, followed by the women and girls. All hold hands, and the line moves in a counterclockwise direction, the dancers using a toe-heel left, toe-heel right step. This goes on for a short while until one of the dancers, usually a man from the head of the line, suddenly bolts from his place, runs to the female portion of the line, and seizes one of the women or girls. Having "stolen" his partner, he swings her around once in place, square-dance style, and then escorts her to the head of the line, where she takes a place directly behind him. The dance then continues as before until another man steals a female partner. Now the women take courage and begin to steal the men and boys, much to the delight of the dancers and spectators. Usually only one or two at a time steal partners. If the group is in a gay mood, partners are stolen from the onlookers as well. There is much whooping during the stealing episodes.

The second figure of the dance has all the dancers turn ninety degrees to the left to face inward forming a circle, still holding hands. They now dance the same heavy hopping step as in the Jump or Stomp Dance, either alternating between left and right feet or on both feet together, moving in a counterclockwise progression, or they dance a few feet in a counterclockwise direction, then reverse to clockwise for a while and then back to counterclockwise as in the Double Head

Illustration 3. Stealing Partners Dance at the Choctaw Fair, Pearl River, Mississippi, 1982. (*Photograph by James Howard*)

or Backward-and-Forward Dance. This figure concludes the dance.

No instrumental accompaniment is used with this dance by the Mississippi Choctaws. The Sixtown Choctaws of Oklahoma use a hand drum.

The Stealing Partners Dance is not mentioned for the Bayou Lacomb Choctaws (Bushnell 1909). Densmore (1943:154–57) presents transcriptions of seven songs of the dance. Although she observed the dance, she does not describe its choreography, stating only that "men and women took part in this dance and (Sidney) Wesley said 'they dance a long time with the first partner and then change to the second.' No further description was obtained. The songs are without instrumental accompaniment" (1943:153).

Drunken-man Dance (*Okishko Hila*) or Goose Dance (*Shalakala Hila*)

At the beginning of this dance the women and girls form a rank, arms linked, on one side of the dance area. The men and boys form a similar rank some distance away, facing the women. The singer stands at one side, keeping time with claves (Mississippi Choctaws) or a hand drum (Oklahoma Choctaws). The tempo of Drunken-man Dance songs is *moderato*. Both men and women join in with the principal singer. The songs are antiphonal, the singer singing a phrase which is answered twice by the dancers. When the song begins, the rank of men advances toward the rank of women using a simple toe-heel left, toe-heel right step. They are all in perfect step and endeavor to keep their rank "dressed" (that is, straight).

When the men's rank has come quite close to that of the women, the women begin to dance forward using the same step and at the same time the men dance backward. When the women have advanced about twenty feet and the men have retreated the same distance, the men dance forward again and the women retreat ahead of them. The two ranks continue backward and forward in this manner for the duration of the dance. At the same time the two ranks are dancing back and forth, the entire group slowly pivots so that the end of the dance usually

Illustration 4. Drunken-man Dance performed by the Choctaw-Chickasaw Heritage Committee near Madill, Oklahoma, 1981. (*Photograph by James Howard*)

finds them ninety degrees counterclockwise of their starting position.

The dance is performed in the same way by all Mississippi Choctaw dance troupes and by Buster Ned's Sixtown Choctaws in Oklahoma. It was not performed by Eugene Wilson's Choctaw dancers in 1974. The narrators for some Mississippi Choctaw dance troupes prefer to call this dance the Goose Dance, and one informant in Mississippi likened the movement of the two ranks of dancers to the wings of a bird in flight. The narrator for the Conehatta community troupe announced this dance as the Corn Dance (*Tanchi Hila*), which is most interesting since the Chickasaws possessed a Corn Dance in which the men and women were in two opposing lines and "when the

lines approached the women were privileged to snatch hand-
kerchiefs or other objects from the men or to pull their hair, and
no resistance could be offered" (Swanton 1928:257).

The various Mississippi Choctaw dance troupes perform the
Drunken-man Dance at different speeds, depending upon the
tempo set by their singer. Some Drunken-man Dance songs
have the dancers, in answering the lead phrase of the singer,
placing a heavy accent at the beginning of the phrase.

Bushnell describes the dance for the Bayou Lacomb Choctaws: "Two lines facing each other are formed by the dancers,
who lock arms. The lines slowly approach, then move backward, and then again approach. All endeavor to keep step,
and during the dance all sing. The song, which is repeated
many times, is evidently a favorite with the Choctaws at Bayou
Lacomb" (1909:21). He does not mention that one rank is made
up exclusively of males, the other exclusively of females, or that
both lines, in their back and forth movement, revolve slowly in
a counterclockwise progression, but it is likely that both features were present.

Densmore (1943:143–49) recorded eight songs of this
dance but did not observe it herself or secure a description of its
choreography.

In my opinion the most common alternative name for this
dance, Goose Dance, was devised to make the dance more
agreeable to white audiences. All of my Choctaw informants,
in both Mississippi and Oklahoma, stressed that the drinking of
alcohol was not associated with the Drunken-man Dance, in
spite of its name, and never had been. The dancers, they said,
merely act "high" or intoxicated. Several tribes of the eastern
United States have a "Drunk" Dance but these are all quite
different in both music and choreography from the Choctaw
Drunken-man Dance. Like the Choctaws, however, the Delawares, Shawnees, Creeks, Seminoles, and Yuchis insist that
drinking alcohol and being inebriated are not a part of their
"Drunk" Dance.

Yelling Dance

This dance I have seen only once, at the rehearsal of the
Bogue Chitto community dance troupe on July 25, 1965. It is

identical in its choreography to the Drunken-man or Goose Dance but has a repetitive tune that all sing in unison. I did not secure a native name for it.

Wedding Dance (*Tumuksila Hila*)

At the beginning of the Wedding Dance several couples, each composed of a man and a woman or a boy and a girl, stand facing each other with their little fingers hooked. They form a circle or a segment of a circle. As the song begins, the men begin dancing forward, the women backwards, thus moving the circle counterclockwise. The step is an oblique step–draw back left, step–draw back right. On musical cue the couples reverse, the women now dancing forward and the men backward. This pattern continues throughout. Both men and women dancers join in answering the lead phrase of the singer. He beats time with claves.

The name of the dance indicates its connection with courtship and marriage. It is a regular feature of the Mississippi Choctaw dance repertoire and was also performed by Eugene Wilson's McCurtain County troupe in 1974. It is not performed by Buster Ned's Sixtown troupe. The narrator for Eugene Wilson's troupe in 1974 explained that in the old days members of the same clan could not dance as couples in the Wedding Dance, reflecting the custom of clan exogamy. The Choctaw Wedding Dance is very similar to, and probably a cognate of, the Shawnee, Delaware, and Oklahoma Seneca-Cayuga Raccoon Dance, except that with these last tribes two men face two women, and there is no linking of little fingers.

The Wedding Dance is probably the dance described by Bushnell as the Bayou Lacomb Choctaw "*Tinsanale Hitkla.*" Of it he writes: "In this dance two persons, facing, clasp each other's hands. Many couples in this position form a ring. One man remains in the center to keep time for the singing and the circle of dancers revolves around him. The Indians say many persons are required in order to perform this dance properly" (Bushnell 1909:21).

Densmore did not find this dance among the Mississippi Choctaws in 1933, though I observed and recorded it in both 1965 and 1974. Curiously, Densmore (1943:113) gives Bushnell's name for this dance, *Tinsanale,* as the name for the Drunken-man Dance, clearly an error.

Chickasaw Garfish Dance (*Nàni Kàlo Hìla*)

This dance is performed by Buster Ned's Choctaw-Chickasaw dance troupe. It is acknowledged by him to be a strictly Chickasaw dance, and usually Bienum Pickens, a Chickasaw member of the troupe, sings for its performance.

Men and women form into pairs for this dance, with the man in front of his partner in the dance line. They proceed single file in a counterclockwise circle using a toe-heel left, toe-heel right step. At the beginning of the strophe proper in the song, the dancers join hands but continue to dance single file. The music for the dance is antiphonal. The singer, after an introductory phrase, sings the lead phrase *we ha yo le,* to which all of the dancers respond *we ha we ha yo le.* After a number of repetitions the singer sings the lead phrase a bit higher, and is answered. This formula is repeated a number of times. At the end of the strophe, as the leader sings the vocables *yo ha,* each couple joins hands and swings twice in place; the second swing

Illustration 5. Chickasaw Garfish Dance performed by the Choctaw-Chickasaw Heritage Committee near Madill, Oklahoma, 1985. (*Photograph by Victoria Lindsay Levine*)

Illustration 6. Chickasaw Garfish Dance, swinging figure, performed by the Choctaw-Chickasaw Heritage Committee near Madill, Oklahoma, 1985. (*Photograph by Victoria Lindsay Levine*)

is incomplete so that the woman finishes in front of the man and thus has a new partner for the next strophe. The dance continues as long as necessary for each woman to dance with each man.

This dance and its accompanying songs are quite similar to the Creek and Seminole Garfish Dance, though neither choreography nor music is completely identical. Buster Ned calls the dance "Hard Fish," and it is listed under that name on the disk *Choctaw-Chickasaw Dance Songs,* vol. 1. The Garfish Dance appears to be the only surviving Chickasaw dance at the present time. The Chickasaws at one time had a repertory of at least twenty-five separate dances, including cognates of the Choctaw Double Head, Duck, Drunken-man, Quail, Raccoon, Snake, Starting, Tick, and Turtle dances and probably the Wedding and War dances (Swanton 1928:257).

War Dance (*Tibuli Hila*) or Drum Dance (*Alepa Hila*)

At the beginning of this dance the men and boys are in a single file at the edge of the dance area, and the women and girls are in a second file just inside that of the men. Each man or

Illustration 7. War or Drum Dance performed by the Choctaw-
Chickasaw Heritage Committee near Madill, Oklahoma, 1985.
(*Photograph by Victoria Lindsay Levine*)

boy is thus paired with the woman or girl on his left. When the
song begins, the dancers move off in a counterclockwise circuit
of the ground. The step employed in this dance varies from
one dance troupe to another. Some troupes employ a martial,
stamping toe-heel right, toe-heel left. Others employ a sort of
skipping step: a quick hop on the left toe followed by a hop on
the left heel, followed by a hop on the right toe and a hop on
the right heel, and so on. Some Mississippi Choctaw troupes
employ the latter step, as do Eugene Wilson's Oklahoma troupe
and Buster Ned's Sixtown Choctaws. Whichever step is used,
the women and girls perform it in a more subdued manner than
the men and boys. On musical cue the men and boys whoop,
and in some troupes they whirl in place, as in the "fancy" Plains
Indian War Dance, then continue as before. Throughout the
dance each male dancer stays to the right of his female partner.

The songs are brisk and martial in nature and of medium
tempo. The singer accompanies himself with claves (Mississippi) or a hand drum (Oklahoma Sixtown Choctaws).

The narrator for performances of the War Dance by Eugene
Wilson's troupe in 1974 commented that of all of the Indian
tribes which perform a War Dance, only the Choctaws admit
female dancers as partners for the men.

Densmore (1943:122–27) recorded five war songs in 1933, but apparently the War Dance was not performed by the Mississippi Choctaws at that time, for she writes: "Sidney Wesley and Mary Hickman danced in the war dances when they were young. There were no wars at that time, but the war dances were held and some of the old songs were sung on those occasions" (Densmore 1943:123). She provides no notes regarding the choreography of the dance.

The War Dance is not mentioned for the Bayou Lacomb Choctaws (Bushnell 1909). Cushman (1899) mentions the Choctaw War Dance but gives no details regarding its performance, saying only that it was "considered important and national" (1899:368). A Choctaw War Dance is also mentioned by the author of the *Relation de la Louisiane,* dating from about 1755 (Swanton 1931:254–55).

Duck Dance (*Okfochush Hiła*)

At the beginning of the Duck Dance the dancers are in a double file, two women facing two men then two more women facing two men, and so on. The men face forward (counterclockwise). When the song begins, the dancers simply tread in place, using a step-draw left, step-draw right. At a change in the song, each pair of women passes under a bridge formed by the joined arms of the pair of men just ahead of them and moves on to the next pair of men. Both men and women quack loudly like ducks as they execute this maneuver, much to the amusement of all present. The dance continues in this manner throughout the song.

In Mississippi the singer for the Duck Dance usually performs *a cappella.* He sometimes performs solo, though the dancers, both men and women, are free to join in if they wish. Adam Sampson, who generally sings for the Duck Dance when it is performed by the Sixtown Choctaws, also performs solo. During the first part of the song he accompanies himself with a single sleigh bell, held in his right hand, but later on he employs a hand drum.

Bushnell describes the Bayou Lacomb Choctaw Duck Dance much as it is still performed in Mississippi and Oklahoma: "Partners are required in this dance also; they form two

Illustration 8. Duck Dance, ducking figure, at the Choctaw Fair,
Pearl River, Mississippi, 1982. (*Photograph by James Howard*)

lines, facing. The peculiar feature is that two partners pass
under the arms of another couple [see illustration 8]. The dancers
endeavor to imitate the motion of a duck in walking, hence the
name of the dance" (1909:21).

Densmore adds a few additional items of information in
her description:

> The action of this dance appears to consist of two parts, each
> imitating ducks. The dancers are in couples, two men holding
> hands and facing two women who also hold each other's hands.
> The men raise their hands and the women stoop and pass under-
> neath, this being "like ducks going under water." The women are
> then face-to-face with two other men who, in turn, raise their
> hands and the women again "dive" underneath. It was also said
> that the dancers *slip* their feet back and forth, at first slowly and
> then faster until the motion is a "fast shuffle." The singer leads in
> the motion. In the songs of the Duck dance . . . the tempo was
> gradually increased to correspond with the motion that has been
> described.

The narrator for the dances performed at the Owa-Chitto
Festival in 1974 explained that this dance was in honor of the

duck, a bird very important to the old-time Choctaws, who used its wing feathers to fletch their arrows and whose meat they often sold to traders.

Several southeastern tribes have cognates of this dance. The Creek and Seminole version is virtually identical to the Choctaw Duck Dance in its choreography. The "Quapaw" dance performed by the Delawares, Shawnees, and Oklahoma Seneca-Cayugas is also very similar, except that among the last three tribes all the dancers continue to move counterclockwise between the "ducking" episodes, and the men, not the women, do the moving to a new position.

Quail Dance (*Kofi Hita*)

In this dance the performers are arranged in two parallel files, women and girls on the inside, men and boys on the out-side. As the song begins, they dance in place with a side-to-side step, that is, right foot pats to left, then returns to right, left foot pats to right and returns, and so on. The leaders of the two files now lead those behind them in a slow counterclockwise progression, still using the same step. On musical cue the dancers in the men's file turn ninety degrees to the left, and those in the

Illustration 9. Quail Dance at the Choctaw Fair, Pearl River, Mississippi, 1982. (*Photograph by James Howard*)

women's file turn ninety degrees to the right, each finding a partner in the opposite file, and begin an alternate hopping on the left
and then the right foot, still moving in a counterclockwise direction. They then face forward as before and do the first step again.
The dance continues in this manner throughout.

The Quail Dance is a favorite among the Mississippi Choctaws, but I have never seen it in Oklahoma. It is not noted for
the Bayou Lacomb Choctaws (Bushnell 1909). Densmore gives
one song of the dance (1943:173) but lumps the description of
its choreography with that of the Terrapin, Turkey, Chicken,
and Pleasure dances. She notes that all of these are danced in
couples and that the dancers move "four times around the
circle, moving in a contraclockwise direction, singing one song.
After circling four times, they begin another song" (1943:172).
She also notes that "a characteristic of the Quail and Duck
dances is a gradual increase in time, possibly associated with
the motion of the birds. The leader sang alone in this dance, and
the songs were accompanied by the striking sticks" (1943:173).

On the evening of July 18, 1974, a young people's dance
troupe from Conehatta community performed a dance, identified by their narrator as the "Friendship Dance," as the first
number in their program. It was identical with the Quail Dance
in its choreography. The same group performed the Quail Dance
(so identified by their narrator) as the seventh number on its
program.

Turtle Dance (*Luksi Hila*)

For the Turtle Dance the men and boys, arms linked, form
in one rank facing the women and girls, who stand in another
rank about twenty feet away, their arms also linked. As the
music begins, the men advance in a straight row toward the
women. Their step is a forward hop on the left foot, holding
the right foot off the ground and slightly to the front. When the
men reach the women's rank, the women begin to hop forward
in the same manner, and at the same time the men begin to hop
backwards. When the two ranks reach the place from which
the men started, the men begin hopping forward again, the
women backwards. The dance continues in this manner until
the end of the song. The song is of medium tempo. Both men

Illustration 10. Turtle Dance at the Owa-Chitto Festival near Broken Bow, Oklahoma, 1974. (*Photograph by James Howard*)

and women join in with the principal singer, who beats time with claves.

The narrator for Eugene Wilson's dance troupe in 1974 explained that this dance was in honor of the turtle, a creature admired by the Choctaws because of its tenacity and long life.

In its choreography the Turtle Dance appears to be a variation of the Drunken-man or Goose Dance. It is danced in the same way in all Mississippi Choctaw communities and likewise by Eugene Wilson's Oklahoma Choctaw troupe. It is not in the repertory of Buster Ned's Sixtown troupe. The Turtle Dance is not among the Bayou Lacomb Choctaw dances described by Bushnell (1909). A Terrapin Dance is described by Densmore (1943:172), but from her account it is not related to the Turtle Dance described above.

Raccoon Dance (*Shawekesa*)

At the beginning of this dance the performers are arranged in a single file, men and boys at the head of the line, women

Illustration 11. Raccoon Dance at the Choctaw Fair, Pearl River, Mississippi, 1974. (*Photograph by James Howard*)

and girls at the rear. All hold hands. The group begins a counter-clockwise circuit of the dance ground using the simple toe-heel left, toe-heel right step. On musical cue one of the men or boys leaves his place in the line and pursues one of the women or girls, who runs through and around the line of dancers, who have stopped in position. Then, suddenly, she turns and begins chasing him, and he just as eagerly attempts to escape.

The music for the Raccoon Dance is antiphonal. The singer sings the lead phrase and is answered by both the men and women dancers.

In 1974 the narrator for the Bogue Chitto dance troupe stated that this dance, particularly the "chase" portion, is in imitation of young raccoons at play. The dance, he said, originated because of the respect the Choctaws had for raccoons, which fight fiercely when cornered.

Bushnell does not mention the dance for the Bayou Lacomb Choctaw (1909), nor is it noted by Densmore (1943). I have seen the dance only in Mississippi, never in Oklahoma.

Snake Dance (*Sinti Hila*)

For the Snake Dance the men and women form a long file, holding hands, all the men first, then the women, with the children at the tail end. As the music begins they commence a serpentine counterclockwise walking progression around the dance area, using a simple toe-heel left, toe-heel right step. The leader, a man, gradually leads the group into a tight spiral formation, then reverses his direction and unwinds the coil of dancers. After straightening out the line, he repeats the same procedure, imitating the coiling and uncoiling of a snake. The dance is a great favorite because the small children at the end of the line tend to be whipped out because they are moving too fast to keep up, and their anxious attempts to retain their footing provide great sport for dancers and spectators alike.

The singer for the Snake Dance stands apart from the dancers. In Mississippi he uses no instrumental accompaniment. The Sixtown Choctaws use a drum. The song for the dance begins at a very slow tempo, both men and women

Illustration 12. Snake Dance, unwinding the coil, at the Choctaw Fair, Pearl River, Mississippi, 1982. (*Photograph by James Howard*)

dancers singing in unison wth the singer. When it is time for the coiling to begin, the singer shouts *we ha,* to which the dancers respond, antiphonally, with *yo yo,* and this call and response pattern continues until the coiling and uncoiling are completed.

At the 1980 Seminole Days celebration, Adam Sampson, singing for Buster Ned's group, stood slightly to one side while singing for the Snake Dance, accompanying himself on a hand drum. Ned, the leader, led the file of dancers into a tight spiral, then out of it and into another, but this time he coiled the "snake" around Sampson so tightly that he finally could not move his arm to hit the drum, which ended the dance. Ned later told me that this maneuver is called "the snake eating a rabbit."

The narrator for the performances of Eugene Wilson's dance troupe in 1974 explained that the Snake Dance was in honor of the snake, particularly the rattlesnake, which was respected as a deity by the old-time Choctaws. Rattlesnakes were not killed by the Choctaws, but they were sometimes captured alive so that their rattles and teeth could be removed. The rattles were fastened at the top of a shaman's rattle to make it sound better and later were put inside the white people's violin for the same reason. The teeth were employed in the scratching tool used to purify individuals in the scratching rite, a part of the annual Green Corn ceremony.

Bushnell's description of the Bayou Lacomb Choctaw performance of the Snake Dance corresponds closely to those I have witnessed in Mississippi and Oklahoma:

> Of the seven dances this appears to have been the great favorite as it was also the last. The dancers form in a single line, either grasping hands or each holding on to the shoulder of the dancer immediately in front. First came the men, then the women, and lastly the boys and girls, if any are to dance. The first man in the line is naturally the leader; he moves in a serpentine course, all following. Gradually he leads the dancers around and around until finally the line becomes coiled, in form resembling a snake. Soon the coil becomes so close it is impossible to move farther; thereupon the participants release their hold on one another and cease dancing. As will be seen, the song belonging to this dance is very simple, but it is repeated many, many times, being sung dur-

ing the entire time consumed by the dance, said to be an hour or more. . . . The snake dance closed the ceremony. [1909:21–22]

Densmore also describes the dance as she witnessed it at Pearl River community in 1933, noting that it was the fourth in the order of dances seen: "Men and women take part in the dance, holding hands in a long line and following a leader. At first they move in sinuous curves, then in a wide circle that gradually narrows until the dancers are in a compact mass with the leader in the middle. By a series of clever maneuvers, he then unfolds the line of dancers until they are again in a long line. . . . The songs among the Choctaw of Mississippi are without instrumental accompaniment" (1943:151–52). She provides transcriptions of two Snake Dance songs (Densmore 1943:152–53).

Bushnell mentions (1909:22) that the Snake Dance invariably ended a night of dancing by the Bayou Lacomb Choctaws, "ending at dawn." It was the final dance at both performances by Eugene Wilson's troupe in 1974, as well. Mississippi Choctaw troupes usually perform the dance near the end of their series of dances, but generally follow it with the War Dance, then exit with the Tick or Walk Dance. This is also true of Buster Ned's Sixtown troupe.

Obsolete Dances

Only those dances currently performed by one or another Choctaw dance troupe have been described above. A few more, still known in the 1930s but now obsolete, are described by Densmore. The first of these is the Bear Dance, and of it she writes: "This was said to be a 'hard jumping dance.' It could be held at any time and the dancers were men and women, moving in couples around the circle and preceded by a leader. The songs were accompanied by the striking sticks carried by the leader who also led the singing and the 'yells,' which were frequently given between renditions of the songs. Wesley . . . said 'when the song goes up higher the dancers step harder and all *holler*'" (Densmore 1943:157). Densmore presents transcriptions of four Bear Dance songs (1943:158–60). She saw the dance performed by a group from Pearl River community (1943:135).

Densmore also describes the Terrapin, Quail, Turkey, Chicken, and Pleasure dances, but she did not see any of them performed, and her data regarding their choreography is self-contradicting:

> The five dances next following may be held at any time. The dancers are in couples, a man and a woman dancing together. They move four times around the circle, moving in a contraclockwise direction, singing one song. After circling four times, they begin another song. The leader of the singing is usually the leader of the dancers, taking his place at the head of the line. However, if he is an old man he is excused from leading the dancers and stands within the circle, singing and beating the striking sticks together to mark the time. The origin of these dances was not ascertained. [Densmore 1943:172]

This paragraph clearly implies that all five dances have the same choreography and differ only in their music. It would also indicate that her "Terrapin Dance," the first of the five, is different from the present-day Choctaw Turtle Dance. The choreographic uniformity of the five dances, however, seems rather unlikely, in view of specific remarks about the last three dances further in her work. For example, regarding the Turkey Dance, she notes: "The step of the Turkey dance consists of a hop with both feet together, first one foot and then the other being placed forward. The song of this dance has words, but their meaning is not known at the present time" (1943:174). And of the Chicken Dance: "The Chicken dance is usually the last dance at a gathering and the dancers do not join in the songs, the leader singing alone" (1943:175).

Densmore's description of the Pleasure Dance flatly contradicts her statement four pages earlier regarding its choreography: "In the Pleasure dance the men are in one row and the women in another row facing them. They move their hands up and down, as though shaking corn in a basket, all moving their hands together. The word yoha means 'shift,' and the men said 'yoha,' the women responding 'ha.' The syllables transcribed with the song are probably adaptations of these words" (1943:176). She presents transcriptions of two Terrapin Dance songs, one Turkey Dance song, one Chicken Dance song, and one Pleasure Dance song (1943:172–73, 174, 175, 176).

Two other obsolete dances are known only from their names, as recorded by Byington in his Choctaw dictionary. These are the Hair Dance (*Paⁿshi Isht Hila*) and the Wolf Dance (*Nashoba Hila*) (Byington 1915:138, 151).

Order of Dances

Before concluding our discussion of Choctaw dances, it is appropriate to comment on the order in which the dances are performed. Bushnell insisted that the dances were always performed in the same unvarying sequence: "The Choctaw living at Bayou Lacomb have one dance ceremony, which is in reality a series of seven distinct dances, performed in rotation *and always in the same order*" (1909:20, italics added). The order Bushnell gives is (1) Man Dance, (2) Tick Dance, (3) Drunken-man Dance, (4) *Tinsanale hitkla,* (5) Duck Dance, (6) Dance Go-and-Come, and (7) Snake Dance (Bushnell 1909:20–22).

Densmore (1943:135) does not mention that the dances must be done in a specific order but does record the order of dances at a gathering she attended at Pearl River Community, this being Tick Dance, Steal-Partner Dance, Bear Dance, and Snake Dance. She adds that "these were followed by the Stomp dance, which was given by request." (Densmore 1943:135) Later she notes that the Chicken Dance was "usually the last dance at a gathering" (1943:175).

Having read Bushnell's statement indicating a strict, unvarying order in the performance of Choctaw dances, and having seen it quoted a number of times by writers on the Choctaws, I took particular care to record the sequence of dances by various Choctaw troupes in Mississippi and Oklahoma. I found no specific order of dances followed in either state. There does seem to be a slight tendency to begin a performance with the Tick Dance and to end with the Snake Dance, but there is no hard and fast rule regarding this.

4. The Songs

The task James Howard assigned me was to transcribe several Choctaw dance songs and, on the basis of these transcriptions, to describe Choctaw traditional music. Since the early publications on Choctaw music by Bushnell (1909) and Densmore (1943), reviewed in Howard's part of the Preface, neither a sizable collection of transcriptions nor a detailed analysis of Choctaw music has been published. Yet significant work on Choctaw music has appeared in recent years. David Draper (1980, 1981, 1982, and 1983), who initiated fieldwork among the Mississippi Choctaws in 1969, rekindled ethnomusicological interest in this repertory after a long hiatus. Martin Fenerty (1981) devoted his doctoral dissertation to a study of traditional music used in elementary classrooms on the Mississippi Choctaw Reservation. My purpose here is to augment these recent contributions by proffering several transcriptions with an updated overview of Choctaw dance songs.

I have drawn my transcriptions and analyses from the materials James Howard originally provided, but my comments represent a larger body of musical and ethnographic data collected during my own fieldwork in 1983 and 1985 (Levine 1990). My information is weighted heavily toward the dance song tradition of the Choctaw-Chickasaw Heritage Committee of Ardmore, Oklahoma. This emphasis reflects the especially generous collaboration afforded me by Heritage Committee members, who are unique among Oklahoma Choctaws. Lack of historical information on the committee has inadvertently led to incorrect assessments of the authenticity of the retentions (Draper 1981) and the sociohistorical influences that have shaped their current performance practices (Lindsay-Levine 1985:141). Therefore their history must be encapsulated here.

The ancestors of committee members removed as a cohesive kin-based community from Mississippi to Indian Territory in 1903 and were resettled near Ardmore in the heart of the Chickasaw Nation. The Ardmore Choctaws, unlike most Oklahoma Choctaws at that time, were all full-bloods, spoke little or no English, and were oriented strongly toward native culture. Several circumstances supported their continuation of traditional lifeways after resettlement, including their isolation from the Choctaw Nation as well as their frontier existence in the remote countryside surrounding Ardmore. Most important, however, at least three Choctaw medicine men and several gifted song leaders were members of this community. One was Logan Parker, a leading elder who specialized in esoteric knowledge and who frequently held ball games and night dances at his home before 1937.

Today, founders of the Choctaw-Chickasaw Heritage Committee retain vivid memories of these early events in which they participated as children and young adults. Buster Ned learned Choctaw culture, music, and dance from his maternal grandfather, Logan Parker. Song leader Adam Sampson also learned from Parker, his maternal uncle, as well as from his father, another prominent singer. Many older members of the committee still speak almost no English, and Choctaw remains the language of preference. They have had only limited contact with other Oklahoma Indians, except for neighboring Chickasaws. Intermarriage with non-Choctaws was extremely rare among the older generation, and they have no connection with the powwow movement. The committee now performs the songs and dances learned through oral tradition directly from their full-blood parents and grandparents, the migrant generation. Committee members have effected superficial changes to adapt the repertory to new performance contexts, but these changes do not differ significantly from the kinds of changes apparent in the current Mississippi repertory. No other Choctaw community now exists in Oklahoma, to my knowledge, that numbers traditional song leaders among its members.

Musical Sources

James Howard's musical sample numbered seventy-six dance songs. His primary sources included the following: (1) two

field recordings by James Howard (Mississippi, 1965); (2) one
field recording by Claude Medford (Mississippi, ca. 1965–70); (3)
American Indian Music of the Mississippi Choctaws, LP (ca. 1974); (4)
Choctaw-Chickasaw Dance Songs, LP (ca. 1979). Selections from
each of these sources appear in the appended transcriptions,
which illustrate the following analysis of Choctaw musical style.
The entire sample consulted for purposes of generalization and
comparison, however, included over three hundred additional
songs from my field recordings, permitting certain conclusions
beyond the confines of the original sample.

Musical Origins, Continuity, and Change

Choctaw dances performed today in Mississippi and Oklahoma constitute what survives of the ball game/night dance
cycle that appeared in many guises among native southeastern
societies. Night dances involved continuous singing and dancing from sundown to sunrise. The cycle could be repeated over
an indefinite period (at least among the Choctaws) lasting from
a few days to a few weeks. As huge public gatherings, these
events provided the main context for social interaction beyond
the domestic circle, but they were also ritual celebrations. The
dances that survive are emblematic of a life that ceased to exist,
for the most part, in the early twentieth century. Yet the values
and cosmology integral to that existence still guide those contemporary Choctaws who are concerned with the preservation
and revitalization of tribal traditions. For these people, the
dances powerfully express social mores and reaffirm group co-
hesion; for outsiders, the dances open a portal on Choctaw culture and demonstrate its ability to endure.

Choctaw singers in Mississippi and Oklahoma transmitted
their repertory for generations through oral tradition. While
one must assume that the repertory underwent considerable
change in style, structure, and content, two bits of evidence
suggest that it also maintained considerable continuity, at least
during this century. The first clue lies in Choctaw attitudes toward musical origins, composition, and change. Buster Ned and
Adam Sampson assert that the dance songs were given to the
Choctaws by supernatural beings at the time of creation. These
same songs are thought to have accompanied Choctaw dances

unchanged throughout the tribe's history. Choctaw-Chickasaw Heritage Committee singers consider the composition of new songs to be impossible; if a song is forgotten, it disappears from the repertory and cannot be replaced.

Obviously, these attitudes toward musical origins, composition, and change are not enough in and of themselves to support academic conclusions regarding the stability of the Choctaw dance song repertory. The concept that no new songs are composed is even contradicted to a degree by a kind of improvisational technique used in dance song performance that involves the variation and recombination of fixed musical materials. In one sense, new dance songs are being composed at each performance. But Choctaw singers insist that the basic musical materials are established and may be varied or recombined only according to convention. They reject the idea that new songs are being composed, although they readily admit that one performance differs from the next. The significant point here is the central role occupied by the concept of continuity in Choctaw musical thought; Choctaws believe that the dance songs have not changed through time. In practice, this concept is reflected in the high priority they place on accurate memorization.

The second clue to consider is found in the comparison of dance songs from Mississippi and Oklahoma. After the removal in 1903, Ardmore-area Choctaws lost all contact with the Mississippi Band of Choctaws until 1977, 1978, and 1979, when members of the Choctaw-Chickasaw Heritage Committee performed at the annual Choctaw Fair in Mississippi. Nevertheless, the two repertories are strikingly parallel; to support this point the appended transcriptions include variant versions of songs from the two locales whenever possible. The similarities retained between the two repertories despite an eighty-year separation, in conjunction with Choctaw concepts of musical origins, composition, and change, support the inference that the dance song repertory has sustained considerable continuity since the turn of the century.

The Song Repertory

Members of the Choctaw-Chickasaw Heritage Committee divide their songs into four main classes: Jump or Stomp dances,

Walk or Tick dances, Drunk dances with related optional dances, and War or Drum dances with related optional dances. The Snake Dance that usually serves as a coda to the performance stands on its own both musically and functionally. Each of the four main categories includes a number of discrete songs identified by a common title and used to accompany one generic choreography. For example, song leader Adam Sampson knows twenty-eight Jump Dance songs, twenty-five Tick Dance songs, nineteen Drunk Dance songs, and seven War Dance songs. (Unfortunately, parallel information on the contemporary dance song repertory in Mississippi is not currently available.) The first two categories, Jump and Tick Dance songs, includes subtypes that alter certain features of either the choreography or the basic musical style; the Starting Dance song and Double Header are considered to be types of Jump Dance songs, while Stealing Partners is thought to be a type of Walk Dance song. The third and fourth categories each include a number of optional dances that may be performed upon request. Sampson includes a Hiding Bullet song, a Wedding song, and a Chickasaw Garfish song in the Drunk Dance category; he classifies Duck, Quail, Bear, and Turtle songs in the War Dance category. Although the songs for the Hiding Bullet, Wedding, Quail, Bear, and Turtle dances remain in the repertory, their choreography has been lost among Heritage Committee members, so they are no longer performed. The optional dances feature certain musical or choreographic similarities to the main category in each case but are not considered subtypes of the main dance. These four main categories, plus the Snake Dance, form the core of contemporary Choctaw dance performances.

The following description and analysis of Choctaw music, along with the appended transcriptions, survey the structure and content of the Choctaw dance song repertory from an ethnic perspective. The scope of this repertory can be very flexible as a result of both regional diversity and compositional practices that remain to be discussed. Therefore, while it is possible to gain a general idea of the repertory's size, structure, and distinctive characteristics, these features remain open-ended.

Choctaw Musical Style

Choctaw dance songs generally employ anhemitonic scales, although half steps do occur in a few songs. The scales include four, five, or six tones each. Each song typically uses a few repetitive rhythmic patterns with frequent changes in meter. Jump Dance and Drunk Dance tempos are moderate, War Dances are fast, while Walk Dances are slow. Most Choctaw dance songs feature call and response; the call is sung by a male song leader and the response is sung by the dancers in unison, with women doubling men at the octave when appropriate. A few of the songs are performed as solos by the male song leader (see transcriptions 20, 21, and 25). Some songs are accompanied by a pair of claves in Mississippi or by a double-headed hand drum in Oklahoma. In either case the percussion instrument is used only to support the song's pulse; it is not used to cue changes in choreography (unlike among other southeastern tribes). Each song concludes with a formulaic call of indefinite pitch, usually employing the vocables "ya ho yo" or "we ha."

While Walk, Drunk, and War Dance songs are quite similar stylistically, Jump Dance songs are distinctive in terms of melody and phrasing. Jump Dance songs characteristically feature level melodic contours that may have a descending inflection. Songs in the other three categories use a variety of melodic contours, including undulating lines, arcs, and inverted arcs. However, descending melodies are most common. The descent may be relatively broad, covering an octave or more, as in example 1. It may be a terraced descent (example 2) or an upward leap followed by an undulating descent (example 3). A descending inflection may be incorporated into a broadly undulating line (example 4).

yo   wi - ta -   ho   ya - le   ya   we - ta

Example 1. Melodic contours: broad descent. Transcription 8 (Walk Dance), measures 5 and 6.

yo da dadiyama yo da-dadiyama yo da-dadiyama yo da- da ya

Example 2. Melodic contours: terraced descent. Transcription 28
(Raccoon Dance), measures 1–4.

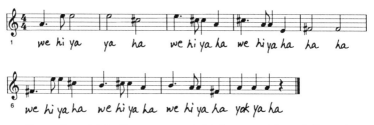

we hi ya   ya   ha   we hi ya ha   we hi ya ha   ha   ha

we hi ya ha   we hi ya ha   we hi ya ha   yok ya ha

Example 3. Melodic contours: initial upward leap followed
by undulating descent. Transcription 21 (Drum Dance),
measures 7–15.

he he ya   ya le ho ya- le he ya   he he ya -   ya le ho ya- le he ya

Example 4. Melodic contours: overall descent incorporated into
broadly undulating line. Transcription 23 (Drum Dance),
measures 5–8.

Phrases in Jump Dance songs tend to be short-winded and
symmetrical, sometimes encompassing no more than one measure; since the melodic contours are often level and rhythmic
patterns are repetitive in these songs, phrases are articulated
through the interplay of vocable patterns within the call and response (see example 5). Phrasing in the other three song categories tends to be longer and more complex, often involving
asymmetrical phrase lengths. Walk Dance songs feature phrases
of one to two and one half measures, Drunk Dance and War
Dance songs sometimes have phrases of three to four measures,
and phrases in some optional dance songs range from one to
five measures (see examples 6 and 7). In Walk, Drunk, and War

Example 5. Jump Dance phrasing and text setting. Transcription 4, opening.

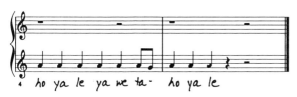

Example 6. Tick or Walk Dance phrasing and text setting. Transcription 9, measures 2–6.

Example 7. Drum or War Dance phrasing and text setting. Transcription 20, measures 12–15.

Dance songs, phrase endings may be articulated through the use of vocal devices such as aspiration and glottal stops or by rests, and the call and response phrases occasionally overlap.

Most Choctaw dance song texts consist of vocable patterns. In Jump Dance songs, a complete vocable pattern encompasses one measure; the number of syllables in each pattern ranges from three to eight, and the vocables are almost always set syllabically (see example 5). Vocable patterns in the other dance song categories also usually comprise one measure, but the pattern is repeated twice or more within a phrase to accommodate its expanded proportions (see example 6). Again, the vocable settings are usually syllabic, but there is a greater tendency to set two notes per syllable in the latter categories, particularly in Walk dances.

The transcriptions presented here include a song from Oklahoma that incorporates two lines of lexical text into the vocable text (see transcription 11) and a song from Mississippi that uses a lexical fragment (see transcription 12). In each case, the lexical items have been transcribed and translated. The Choctaw-Chickasaw Heritage Committee now employs lexical texts in some 20 percent of their songs. As in transcription 11, the lexical lines are always framed by vocables and are usually sung by the leader alone, although in a few songs the chorus also sings lexical lines. The dance song category determines the textual content; Jump Dance songs use slapstick texts, Walk Dance songs feature serious or reflective texts, Drunk Dance songs are ironic or mildly chastening, and War Dance songs are reflective. No parallel information on the use of lexical texts is available at present for Mississippi Choctaws.

Musical Form and Design

The predominant Choctaw compositional principle, variation, produces an assortment of song forms and designs. Previous researchers have described Choctaw song structures as period form (Densmore 1943:118), sectional (Draper 1980:154), or strophic (Draper 1983:291). The analyses here attempt to elaborate upon these characterizations and have been informed by elicitations of Ned and Sampson's music theory. Four main forms appear in Choctaw songs; I call them Jump Dance, chant, refrain, and strophic form. Each is discussed in turn.

Jump Dance Form

Jump Dance form is found primarily in Jump Dance songs, which usually last no longer than a minute. Jump Dance songs employ the simplest form in Choctaw music, stringing together several short, repetitive phrases in succession. They generally are not tuneful songs. Rather, they are characterized by a dynamically accented articulation of the beat and are propelled by clear, strong rhythms, including some syncopations. In generic songs of this category, as illustrated in example 8, the leader varies one call phrase throughout the song or alternates two or more phrases that contrast slightly in terms of rhythm, vocables, or melodic inflection. The chorus responds with one fixed phrase throughout, although the pitch level of the response may move up or down a step according to the final note of the preceding call. The call and response each constitute one measure. The response phrase is related to the initial call, duplicating all or part of the call's vocable or rhythmic patterns; it may contrast with the call by using a different melodic inflection. The meter of the call may differ from that of the response; similarly, the meters of various calls used in any given song may differ from one another.

The Jump Dance category includes two subtypes, the Starting Dance and the Double Header, each of which modifies basic Jump Dance form. In the Starting Dance (example 9), the call consists of one to three notes; the chorus responds first with one note and later echoes the leader. Each sequence repeats several times before the leader introduces the next call in the series. The call and response pair always comprises one phrase, encompassing a single measure. The response occasionally differs from the call but it is not highly contrastive. The Starting Dance song sounds something like Creek and Cherokee Stomp Dance songs.

The Double Header (see example 10), like the Starting Dance, alternates several short call patterns with the response, and the call-response pair comprises one phrase, encompassing one measure. However, in the Double Header, the response employs one vocable pattern throughout the song, as in stan-

Example 8. Standard Jump Dance form. Transcription 5, measures 1–7.

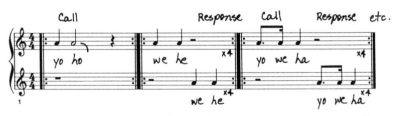

Example 9. Starting Dance form. Transcription 1, measures 1–3.

Example 10. Double Header Dance form. Transcription 7, measures 4–7.

dard Jump Dance songs. Again, the pitch level of the response may adjust to the final note of the previous call.

Elements of Jump Dance form also appear in two dances from outside the category: the Quail and Snake Dance songs. In the Quail Dance song (see transcription 26), the leader repeats a single call that alternates with one of two closely related choral responses. The call and response pair form one phrase, and the complete sequence comprises a two-phrase unit encompassing four measures. This part is set against a second ensemble that performs a counterpoint like that of a Starting Dance. The first ensemble alternates triple and common meter while the counter ensemble sustains common meter, producing a kind of rhythmic polyphony not otherwise found in Choctaw songs and generally rare in American Indian music. The Snake Dance (see transcription 30) consists of two contrasting sections. The first section (measures 1 through 5) approximates an especially tuneful Jump Dance; the second section (beginning in measure 6), which accompanies the "coiling" choreography, is like a Double Header Dance song.

Chant Form

All Walk Dance songs employ chant form, which is also found in most of the Choctaw-Chickasaw Heritage Committee's Drunk Dance songs. Songs in chant form differ in several respects from those in Jump Dance form. In chant-form songs, the calls and responses are longer, often encompassing two or more measures each. These phrases are more complex and are expanded through internal repetition of all or part of the melodic and vocable patterns. In some cases an antecedent-consequent relationship is established, in a melodic sense, between the call and response phrases. The calls and responses may change meter frequently, which results in asymmetrical phrase lengths and sometimes obscures the pulse. The last note of the response may overlap with the first note of the subsequent call. Finally, the melodic contours in chant-form songs contribute to the articulation of phrases and larger formal divisions within the song. Example 11 typifies chant-form songs.

Songs in chant form are sectional. The number of sections in any given chant-form song depends upon the number of different chants found in its choral response. The song leader de-

Example 11. Chant form: Stealing Partners Dance. Transcription 13, measures 1–5, 10–15, 19–24.

termines the number of chants used and their arrangement in a performance. The chants that may be used successively within one song are fixed; only certain chants may be used with certain other chants, and they must be used in a predetermined order. Within these guidelines a chant may be repeated an indefinite number of times before the song leader cues a change in the chant. Chant-form songs may use from one to five different chants, although most songs employ two or three. For example, the Stealing Partners song (example 11), a type of Walk Dance, uses three different chants. Once the leader changes the chant, the preceding chant or chants are not repeated. The chants within one song are differentiated from each other by vocable and rhythmic patterns, meters, and melodic contours, or some combination of these features.

The chorus repeats its response unvaried throughout any given song section in chant form, while the song leader subjects his call to melodic and rhythmic permutations. The leader may repeat or alternate improvised variations indefinitely within each section of the song. To illustrate, the Stealing Partners song (example 11) is diagrammed in figure 1. The leader achieved formal symmetry in this particular rendition through the use of the same number of varied calls in the outer two song sections, but he would not necessarily reproduce this design in subsequent performances of Stealing Partners.

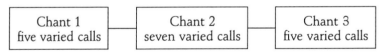

Fig. 1. Chant-form Song, Stealing Partners Dance
(see transcription 13)

Chant form is highly plastic, both within each section of a song and in the overall design of a song. The song leader sustains musical interest by constant variation of his calls, yet the chorus maintains unity within each section by constant repetition of the chant response. The form permits the construction of relatively long performances of a single song. Contemporary Walk Dance performances in Oklahoma, for example, may last five minutes or more, but in earlier times a single Walk Dance song could last longer than half an hour. Additionally, each performance of a given chant-form song differs from the next. It is in this sense that the song leader improvises on fixed materials, generating continually fresh interpretations.

Refrain Form

Refrain form is found primarily in War Dance and optional dance songs. In refrain form songs, the call and response together comprise a verse that alternates with a call and response refrain. The refrain may be repeated an indefinite number of times before the verse returns, as in example 12. A variation on this design involves the use of two alternating verse melodies, as in the Duck Dance song (example 13). In this song, either melody of the verse may alternate with the refrain, and the refrain may be repeated two or three times between each verse. The recurrence of the verse cues the dancers to perform the

Example 12. Refrain form: Drunken-man Dance. Transcription 15, measures 5–14.

Example 13. Refrain form: Duck Dance. Transcription 24, measures 8–13, 16–17.

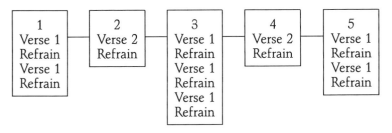

Fig. 2. Refrain-form Song, War Dance (see transcription 20)

"passing" maneuver in the choreography. An unusual refrain design that employs two alternating verse melodies appears in the War Dance song (transcription 20). The alternation of verse and refrain in this song creates a symmetrical, five-part palindrome structure, outlined in figure 2. In these three songs, as in refrain-form songs generally, the verses are set at a higher pitch than the refrains, leading several scholars to point out the use of rise form in some Choctaw songs.

Strophic Form

Strophic forms occur in a few Drunk Dance and War Dance songs as well as in the Chickasaw Hard Fish or Gar Dance. These forms are similar to the kinds of strophic forms found among other southeastern tribes. In most cases they feature an introduction followed by a fixed strophe; the strophe alone is repeated many times and constitutes the body of the song. The strophic forms as a whole exhibit the greatest variety in design and may employ frequent changes in texture, tempo, or melodic style. These alternations coincide with changes in choreography. The War or Drum Dance song (transcription 23) and the Chickasaw Hard Fish Dance (transcription 19) illustrate strophic form.

The Drum Dance of transcription 23 is introduced with three call and response phrases. Then the strophe proper is sung once by the chorus and song leader in unison. Subsequent repetitions of the strophe are performed in call and response. This particular strophic design is unique to the Drum Dance of transcription 23, which was led only by the late Ardis Mose. The Chickasaw Hard Fish Dance, by contrast, opens with a relatively slow, free solo performed by the song leader that concludes with a brief call and response passage. The tempo increases significantly at the beginning of the strophe, which contains two contrasting sections. The strophe in the Hard Fish Dance opens with a relatively long call and response section, similar in style to a standard Jump Dance song, and concludes with a brief section that resembles a Double Header Dance song.

Conclusions

The four basic forms found in Choctaw dance songs sustain a rich, diverse repertory that displays a subtle balance between repetition and variation. Traditional Choctaws complement their interest in musical continuity with a desire for individuality among song leaders as well as among dance troupes from different communities. Many of the apparent differences between the music of Mississippi and Oklahoma Choctaws reflect this penchant for regional diversity rather than any substantive divergence in style or repertory. Contemporary performances by various Mississippi Choctaw troupes differ from one another as well as from those of the Oklahoma Choctaw-Chickasaw Heritage Committee, but these differences involve primarily superficial aspects of performance practice. For example, when Mississippi Choctaws use striking sticks for percussive accompaniment, the Heritage Committee employs a hand drum, yet the style and function of that accompaniment remains unchanged. Mississippi Choctaw dance troupes tend to standardize and coordinate their costumes, whereas Heritage Committee dancers interpret "traditional dress" in highly individualistic ways. These kinds of differences ultimately have little bearing on the actual content of any given performance or on the musical repertory as a whole. Rather, dance performances in both Mississippi and Oklahoma attest to the continuity of certain domains of traditional Choctaw culture, adapted and reinterpreted to fit new circumstances but still vital despite the fierce pressure to assimilate that both groups have endured.

Musical Transcriptions

These transcriptions are intended to illustrate the description and analysis of Choctaw dance songs in chapter 4, as well as for use as source material in conjunction with the available recordings. I have used standard Western notation for the sake of convenience, but the transcriptions do not capture all the tonal and rhythmic nuances inherent in this repertory. For example, the formulaic calls that conclude many of the songs are of indefinite pitch, as are some notes in the Jump Dance songs. The pitches transcribed here are only approximate in these cases. In addition, many of the transcriptions present only the song's basic musical phrases, omitting the variations and repetitions in the interest of economy. The songs are notated in treble clef but are sung an octave lower. The song leader's part appears in the top staff, with the choral part in the bottom staff. The pulse is supported in many songs by a drum (Oklahoma) or striking sticks (Mississippi), which are not indicated here. In James Howard's field recordings, the late Ida Mae Frazer sings with Prentis Jackson as a co-leader, doubling his line at the octave but delaying her entry by one or two beats on the calls. This is reflected in some, but not all, of my transcriptions, as I chose to highlight call and response texture where possible. Diacritics used here include: (♩), note sung slightly after the beat; +, pitch sung about one-quarter tone higher than written;), falling release; and x4, number of repetitions.

Transcription 1. Starting Dance (Mississippi)

SOURCE: Howard field recording, 1965; Prentis Jackson, song leader.

Transcription 2. Jump Dance (Oklahoma)

SOURCE: *Choctaw-Chickasaw Dance Songs,* LP, vol. 1, ca. 1979; Adam Sampson, song leader.

Transcription 3. Jump Dance (Mississippi)

SOURCE: Howard field recording, 1965; Prentis Jackson, song leader.

Transcription 4. Jump Dance (Mississippi)

SOURCE: Howard field recording, 1965; Henry Joe, song leader.

Transcription 5. Jump Dance (Oklahoma)

SOURCE: *Choctaw-Chickasaw Dance Songs,* LP, vol. 1, ca. 1979; Adam
Sampson, song leader.

Transcription 6. Double Header Dance (Mississippi)

SOURCE: Medford field recording, ca. 1965–70; song leader unknown.

Transcription 7. Double Header Dance (Oklahoma)

SOURCE: *Choctaw-Chickasaw Dance Songs,* LP, vol. 2, ca. 1979; Adam
Sampson, song leader.

SOURCE: Howard field recording, 1965; Prentis Jackson and Ida Mae
Frazer, song leaders.

Transcription 9. Tick Dance (Oklahoma)

SOURCE: *Choctaw-Chickasaw Dance Songs,* LP, vol. 1, ca. 1979; Adam
Sampson, song leader.

Transcription 10. Walk Dance (Mississippi)

SOURCE: Howard field recording, 1965; Prentis Jackson and Ida Mae Frazier, song leaders.

NOTE: This song is entitled "Losing Wife Song" on the LP recording *American Indian Music of the Mississippi Choctaws,* vol. 2, side 1.

Transcription 11. *Palata* or Tick Dance (Oklahoma)

yo we- le   ya   yo- we- le - ya   ha

SOURCE: *Choctaw-Chickasaw Dance Songs,* LP, vol. 2, ca. 1979; Adam Sampson, song leader.

NOTE: The text and translation for this song are as follows:

Text	Translation
Ya kut unta le ma	This is what I was doing
ohoyo ut akiania	when I lost my woman
yo me kia na ne	but now I don't feel a thing.
isa kanimi.	

This text was transcribed and translated by Buster Ned, who interprets the song as meaning that the narrator was dancing when his wife died, and as a result of her loss he feels emotionally devastated.

Transcription 12. Stealing Partners Dance (Mississippi)

SOURCE: Howard field recording, 1965; Prentis Jackson and Ida Mae
Frazer, song leaders.
NOTE: The text in measure 9 is *ho ohi itimolobe,* which refers to "stealing"
a partner from among the dancers.

Transcription 13. Stealing Partners Dance (Oklahoma)

SOURCE: *Choctaw-Chickasaw Dance Songs,* LP, vol. 2, ca. 1979; Adam
Sampson, song leader.

Transcription 14. Drunk Dance (Mississippi)

SOURCE: Howard field recording, 1965; Henry Joe and Ida Mae Frazer, song leaders.

Transcription 15. Drunk Dance (Mississippi)

SOURCE: Howard field recording, 1965; Prentis Jackson and Ida Mae
Frazer, song leaders.

Transcription 16. Drunk Dance (Oklahoma)

SOURCE: *Choctaw-Chickasaw Dance Songs,* LP, vol. 2, ca. 1979; Ardis Mose, song leader.

Transcription 17. Drunk Dance (Oklahoma)

SOURCE: *Choctaw-Chickasaw Dance Songs,* LP, vol. 2, ca. 1979; Adam
Sampson, song leader.

Transcription 18. Wedding Dance (Mississippi)

SOURCE: Howard field recording, 1965; Prentis Jackson and Ida Mae Frazer, song leaders.

Transcription 19. Chickasaw Hard Fish Dance (Oklahoma)

SOURCE: *Choctaw-Chickasaw Dance Songs,* LP, vol. 1, ca. 1979; Bienum Pickens, song leader.

Transcription 20. War Dance (Mississippi)

SOURCE: Howard field recording, 1965; Prentis Jackson, soloist.
NOTE: The tempo accelerates to ♩ = 180 by the conclusion of the song.

Transcription 21. Drum Dance (Oklahoma)

SOURCE: *Choctaw-Chickasaw Dance Songs,* LP, vol. 2, ca. 1979; Adam Sampson, soloist.

Transcription 22. War Dance (Mississippi)

SOURCE: Howard field recording, 1965; Prentis Jackson and Ida Mae Frazer, song leaders.

Transcription 23. Drum Dance (Oklahoma)

SOURCE: *Choctaw-Chickasaw Dance Songs,* LP, vol. 2, ca. 1979; Ardis Mose, song leader.

NOTE: The chorus is tacet during the first four measures, entering only on the repeat.

Transcription 24. Duck Dance (Mississippi)

SOURCE: Medford field recording, ca. 1965–70; song leader unknown.

Transcription 25. Duck Dance (Oklahoma)

SOURCE: *Choctaw-Chickasaw Dance Songs,* LP, vol. 1, ca. 1979; Adam
Sampson, soloist.

Transcription 26. Quail Dance (Mississippi)

SOURCE: *American Indian Music of the Mississippi Choctaws,* LP, vol. 1, 1974; Tony Bell, Prentis Jackson, and Henry Joe, song leaders.

NOTE: The counter chant shown in the third staff requires additional explanation. It should be in 4/4 throughout so that the metric bars do not coordinate with the other parts. Unfortunately, this was impossible with the music notation software used to prepare the transcriptions. An upward stem in the third staff indicates the counter-leader's call, while a downward stem indicates the dancers' response.

Transcription 27. Turtle Dance (Mississippi)

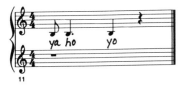

SOURCE: Howard field recording, 1965; Prentis Jackson and Ida Mae Frazer, song leaders.

Transcription 28. Raccoon Dance (Mississippi)

SOURCE: Howard field recording, 1965; Prentis Jackson and Ida Mae
Frazer, song leaders.

Transcription 29. Snake Dance (Mississippi)

SOURCE: Howard field recording, 1965; Prentis Jackson, song leader.

Transcription 30. Snake Dance (Oklahoma)

SOURCE: *Choctaw-Chickasaw Dance Songs,* LP, vol. 1, ca. 1979; Adam Sampson, song leader.

Sources Cited

Blanchard, Kendall
1981 *The Mississippi Choctaws at Play: The Serious Side of Leisure.* Urbana: University of Illinois Press.
Bushnell, David I.
1909 *The Choctaw of Bayou Lacomb, St. Tammany Parish, Louisiana.* Bureau of American Ethnology Bulletin 48. Washington, D.C.: Government Printing Office.
Byington, Cyrus
1915 *A Dictionary of the Choctaw Language.* Bureau of American Ethnology Bulletin 46. Washington, D.C.: Government Printing Office.
Catlin, George
1844 *Letters and Notes on the Manners, Customs, and Conditions of the North American Indians Written During Eight Year's Travel (1832–1839) Amongst the Wildest Tribes of Indians in North America,* Vol. 2. London.
1913 *North American Indians,* Vols. 1 and 2. Philadelphia.
Colvin, Thomas A.
1978 *Cane and Palmetto Basketry of the Choctaws of St. Tammany Parish, Lacombe, Louisiana.* Ed. Melba Elfer Colvin. Mandeville, La.: Daybreak Publishing Company.
Cushman, H. B.
1962 *History of the Choctaw, Chickasaw and Natchez Indians.* Ed. Angie Debo. New York, N.Y.: Russell and Russell.
Densmore, Frances
1932 *Menominee Music.* Bureau of American Ethnology Bulletin 102. Washington, D.C.: Government Printing Office.
1943 *Choctaw Music.* Bureau of American Ethnology Bulletin 136. Washington, D.C.: Government Printing Office.
1956 *Seminole Music.* Bureau of American Ethnology Bulletin 161. Washington, D.C.: Government Printing Office.
Draper, David E.
1980 "Occasions for the Performance of Native Choctaw Music." *Selected Reports in Ethnomusicology* 3:147–73.
1981 Review of *Choctaw-Chickasaw Dance Songs. Ethnomusicology* 29 (3): 553–56.

1982   Review of *American Indian Music of the Mississippi Choctaws. Ethnomusicology* 26 (2):333–37.
1983   "Breath in Music: Concept and Practice Among the Choctaw Indians." *Selected Reports in Ethnomusicology* 4:285–300.
Fenerty, Martin William
1981   "An Attitudinal Survey of Southern Choctaws on Traditional Amerindian Music in Early Childhood Education." Ph.D. diss., University of Mississippi.
Howard, James H.
1955   "Pan-Indian Culture of Oklahoma." *Scientific Monthly* 81 (5):215–20.
1961   "Cultural Persistence and Cultural Change as Reflected in Oklahoma Seneca-Cayuga Ceremonialism." *Plains Anthropologist* 6 (11): 21–30.
1965   *The Ponca Tribe.* Bureau of American Ethnology Bulletin 195. Washington, D.C.: Government Printing Office.
1968   *The Southeastern Ceremonial Complex and Its Interpretation.* Memoir Number 6. Columbia: Missouri Archaeological Society.
1976   "Oklahoma Choctaw Revive Native Dances." *Actes du XLIIe Congrès International des Americanistes* 5:315–23.
1981   *Shawnee! The Ceremonialism of a Native American Tribe and Its Cultural Background.* Athens: Ohio University Press.
Kurath, Gertrude P.
1981   *Tutelo Rituals on Six Nations Reserve, Ontario.* Special Series Number 5. Ann Arbor, Mich.: The Society for Ethnomusicology.
Levine, Victoria Lindsay
1989   "Choctaw Indian Musical Cultures in the Twentieth Century." Ph.D. diss. (musicology), University of Illinois–Urbana.
Lindsay-Levine, Victoria J.
1990   "Duck Dance." In Bruno Nettl, *The Western Impact on World Music: Change, Adaptation, and Survival,* pp. 139–41. New York, N.Y.: Schirmer Books.
Milligan, Dorothy.
1976   *The Indian Way, Chickasaws.* Quanah, Texas: Nortex Press.
Ned, Buster
n.d.   *Choctaw-Chickasaw Dance Songs* (LP), Vols. 1 and 2. Oklahoma City, Oklahoma: Choctaw-Chickasaw Heritage Committee.
Speck, Frank G.
1942   *The Tutelo Spirit Adoption Ceremony: Reclothing the Living in the Name of the Dead.* Harrisburg, Pa.: Publications of the Pennsylvania Historical Commission.
1955   *The Iroquois: A Study in Cultural Evolution.* Bulletin 23. Bloomfield Hills, Mich.: Cranbrook Institute of Science.
Speck, Frank G. and Leonard Broom, in collaboration with Will West Long
1951   *Cherokee Dance and Drama.* Berkeley: University of California Press.

Swanton, John R.
1928   *Social and Religious Beliefs and Usages of the Chickasaw Indians.* Bureau of American Ethnology, 49th Annual Report, pp. 167–273. Washington, D.C.: Government Printing Office.
1931   *Source Material for the Social and Ceremonial Life of the Choctaw Indians.* Bureau of American Ethnology Bulletin 103. Washington, D.C.: Government Printing Office.
1946   *The Indians of the Southeastern United States.* Bureau of American Ethnology Bulletin 137. Washington, D.C.: Government Printing Office.

Tanner, John
1830   *A Narrative of the Captivity and Adventures of John Tanner.* New York, N.Y.: G. & C. H. Carvill.

Timberlake, Lt. Henry
1948   *Memoirs of Lieut. Henry Timberlake 1756–1765.* Ed. Samuel Cole Williams. Marietta, Ga.: Continental Book Company.

Wright, Muriel H.
1951   *A Guide to the Indian Tribes of Oklahoma.* Norman: University of Oklahoma Press.

Index

African-American influence on the Choctaws: 24–25
Alabama Indians: 36
Antiphonal singing: 37, 38, 39, 40, 42–43, 46, 50, 58, 69
"Apafalaya" chief: 3
"Apafalaya" (Mississippi) River: 3
Appliqué designs: 34–35
Apushmataha (Mississippi Choctaw Chief): 3

Backward-and-Forward Dance: 41; see also Double Head Dance
Ball game: see stickball game
Ball game/night dance cycle: 66
Ball Play Dance: 7, 10
Baptist Church: 6
Bayou Lacomb Choctaws (Louisiana): 20, 21, 28, 38, 40, 46, 48, 49, 53, 56, 57, 58, 60, 61, 63; drum of, 23–24
Beadwork designs: 35–36
Bear Dance: 61, 63; song for, 68
Bell, Tony: 15
Bells: 20, 27–29, 33, 53
Belvin, James: 13
Blanchard, Kendall: 1, 25–26, 30
Bogue Chitto, Mississippi: 15, 17, 24, 27, 28, 38; dance troupes from, 17, 39, 40, 41, 43, 48, 58
Bogue Houma, Mississippi: 17
Borrow Money Dance: 40, 41; see also Jump Dance
Bureau of Indian Affairs: 5
Bushnell, David I.: 21, 23–24, 28,

38, 40, 42, 48, 49, 53, 57, 58, 60, 61, 63, 64
Byington, Cyrus: 63

Cajuns: 31
Catlin, George: 7, 12, 33; description of Oklahoma Choctaw stickball game and dances, 7–12
Cayuga Indians: 22
Chanter: 21; see also song leaders
Chant form in Choctaw songs: 73, 75–78; musical example of, 76
Cherokee Indians: 22, 27, 32, 36, 38
Chickasaw Indians: 3, 15, 47, 65; dance repertory of, 51
Chickasaw Nation: 65
Chicken Dance: 56, 62, 63
Choctaw-Chickasaw Heritage Committee: 13, 15, 16, 20, 22, 23, 28, 32, 33, 39, 42, 43, 46, 47, 49, 50, 52, 53, 57, 59, 60, 61, 64, 65, 67, 72, 75, 81; founding of, 15–16
Choctaw Fair (Mississippi): 15, 17, 18–19, 20, 27, 30, 38, 40; dance performances at, 17–18; compared to Pan-Indian Powwows, 18–19
Choctaw General Council (Oklahoma): 6, 7
Choctaw Indian Agency (Mississippi): 5
Choctaw Nation (Oklahoma): 6, 65

13, 60; Creek and Seminole, 19;
Yuchi, 27

Hair Dance: 63
Hard Fish Dance (Chickasaw):
50–51; illustrations of, 50, 51;
song for, 68, 80
Henry, Bob, 24, 27, 30, 40
Henry, Robert: 24, 29
Hiding Bullet Song: 68
Horned serpent: 36
House Dances: 18

Improvisation in Choctaw songs:
77; *see also* composition of
Choctaw songs
Indian Awareness: 14
Indian Territory: 6, 65

Jackson, Prentis: 18, 38, 39, 40,
43–44, 83
Jena Choctaws (Louisiana): 15
Joe, Henry: 38
Joe, Ovie: 38
Jump Dance: 21, 22, 37, 38, 39–41,
42, 45, 67; illustration of, 40;
songs for, 69, 70, 72, 73–75, 80,
83; musical example of, 71, 74

Kiowa Indians: 14

Link Arms Dance: 40; *see also*
Jump Dance
Long Hairs: 3
Louisiana Choctaws: 6, 22, 27, 33;
see also Bayou Lacomb Choc-
taws and Jena Choctaws
Louisiana Indians: 5
Louisiana Purchase (1803): 3

Man Dance: 41, 63; *see also* Jump
Dance
Melody in Choctaw songs: 69
Menominee Indians: 21, 22
Methodist Church: 6

Mississippian archaeological cul-
ture: 36
Mississippi Choctaws: 3, 4–5, 19,
39, 42, 44, 46, 47, 56, 64, 72;
music education among, 64
Mississippi Territory: 3–4
Mohawk Indians: 22
Morris, Wilson: 28
Mose, Ardis: 80
Musical form in Choctaw songs:
72–80
Musical instruments of the Choc-
taws: 20–30
Muskhogean Indians: 19

Ned, Buster: 13, 16, 22, 23, 34–
35, 65, 72; biography of, 15;
dance troupe of, *see* Choctaw-
Chickasaw Heritage Committee
Night dances: 65

Ojibway Indians: 22
Oklahoma Choctaws: 6–16, 42
Oneida Indians: 22
Onondaga Indians: 22
Origins of Choctaw music: 66
Owa-Chitto Festival (Broken Bow,
Oklahoma): 15, 54

"Pafallaya" province (Missis-
sippi): 3
Pan-Indian influence on the Choc-
taws: 14, 22, 23, 32, 34
Pa^{n}s-falaya: 3
Parker, Logan: 13, 15, 65
Pearl River, Mississippi: 17, 61,
62, 63
Phrasing in Choctaw songs: 70
Pickens, Bienum: 16, 23, 50
Plains Indians: 14, 28, 52; influence
on the Choctaws, *see* Pan-Indian
influence on the Choctaws
Pleasure Dance: 56, 62
Ponca Indians: 14
Prairie Indians: 28